THE KILLING HANDBOOK

THE KILLING HANDBOOK

FORBRYDELSEN FOREVER!

EMMA KENNEDY

First published in Great Britain in 2012 by the
Orion Publishing Group
an imprint of the Orion Publishing Group Ltd
Orion House, 5 Upper St Martin's Lane, London, WC2H 9EA

1 3 5 7 9 10 8 6 4 2

A CIP catalogue record for this book is
available from the British Library.

ISBN: 9781409109235

The Orion Publishing Group Ltd
Orion House
5 Upper St Martin's Lane
London WC2H 9EA

An Hachette UK Company

Photography © Tine Harden

Printed by
CPI Group (UK) Ltd, Croydon, CR0 4YY

www.orionbooks.co.uk

For Neil, who loves *The Killing* as much as I do

CONTENTS

FOREWORD
by Sophie Gråbøl

I am writing this the day after the very last shoot of *The Killing 3*. Which was also the very last day of all *The Killing*, since both Søren Sveistrup and I are determined not to take Sarah Lund through any more dark journeys, risking life and limb in the chase of a killer. She's been through enough!

The last weeks of shooting have been more stressful than ever; with writers, cast and crew giving their all for the last finale, and – as always with this project – in a race against time. Being so focused on getting all the last scenes home, there hasn't really been time to reflect much about how it would be to say goodbye to our safe little world of darkness and murder, to which I've belonged for seven years. Consequently, it hits me like a tsunami today, how much I love being a part of *The Killing*, and how much I'm going to miss it.

I'll miss the strong sense of loyalty and togetherness with an amazing, hard-working team. I'll miss the incredible commitment from all the great actors involved, all of us standing on our toes to make each other better – a rare feeling of an ensemble, telling the story together. I'll miss the hours in the writer's room, our war-room, where the very heart of the series is based. A tiny room, but yet the most spacious in terms of discussions and ideas, arguments and laughter. Maybe that's what I'll miss the most.

I think all of us involved in *The Killing* take an almost parental pride in the project, and to see it so well received outside of Denmark has been such a joy. Especially the way it has been understood and embraced in the UK has been totally overwhelming. Actually, the only thing that keeps me from moving to England in a second, is the fear of ending my days tied up in the basement of Emma Kennedy's house. My God, this woman is obsessed. At first it was flattering to experience her fascination with Sarah Lund; here was a true fan, who was into every aspect of the character. She could tell me how Sarah Lund behaved in every detail, like for instance "Sarah Lund never says goodbye on the phone". "Sarah Lund always has a little smile in the corner of her mouth, if she thinks someone is guilty", hundreds of little things like that. Pretty quickly I became aware that this was not only a kind observation, it was more like a law to obey, an order to follow. I started feeling guilty every time I did say goodbye on the phone, or forgot the little smile. Soon it became plain frightening, when I realized that this Emma Kennedy wasn't a woman to not obey. She even slapped me on my arm at one time. Hard! And they say the Danes have no manners...

I hope this book will be enjoyed. And I hope it will have some cathartic effect on Emma, so she can move on with her life. And leave me alone. Please, Emma.

Sofie Gråbøl, Copenhagen, September 2012

INTRODUCTION

Forbrydelsen Fever

Hej! Have you been experiencing an inexplicable longing for rain and long, dark nights? Developed an overwhelming urge to pull on a slightly itchy-looking jumper and frown a lot? There's no need to panic. You have *Forbrydelsen* Fever. Congratulations.

A virus has swept the Great British islands, blown in on a north wind; and it has brought with it the murky Nordic Noir televisual blockbusters that have gripped the nation ever since.

But one series has risen above the others, its murderous majesty sweeping aside everything in its path. It's gritty, it's methodical, it's packed with bananas and it has the greatest female character ever created: Sarah Lund.

Sarah Lund is, quite simply, the total bees' knees. We've had female detectives before: there was Cagney and Lacey, the wise-cracking duo who ate bagels dangerously and wore plaid A-line skirts with a sense of reckless abandon. In Britain, we had Miss Marple, the quintessential English busybody, who somehow managed to solve fiendish crimes in leafy settings over a cream tea with nothing more than a sharp eye and an ear for gossip. We then moved up a notch with Jane Tennison, the difficult and demanding boss of an all-male team who cracked cases while sporting a pencil skirt and some natty high heels; but not even Dame Helen Mirren and her impossibly sexy legs can hold a candle to the incomparable Danish detective.

So let's celebrate Sarah Lund and everything *Forbrydelsen*. It's the greatest show on telly and I will wrestle anyone who says differently.

This book is your step-by-step guide to everything you're going to need to pretend you are Danish, bone up on everything suspicious and transform yourself into Sarah Lund herself.

You're going to learn Danish, eat Danish food, study Danish history; you're going to wrap your noggin round the subtle intricacies of Danish politics (TROOOOOOEEEEELLLLLS), throw yourself into dating Danish-style, transform your living space into Danish interior design heaven, knit a jumper, wear it – and then, and only then, you can travel to Copenhagen, track down all the locations and shout 'Tak!' at the top of your voice.

Not only that, but I'm going to explain every single plot hole you've ever wondered about, give you a sneaky peek into the mysteries of Series 3 and, if you dare, you can take on the Ultimate *Forbrydelsen* Quiz that even cast members are terrified of. Let's go! *Forbrydelsen* for ever!

✳︎⚬✳︎⚬✳︎ 1 ✳︎⚬✳︎⚬✳︎

SO YOU WANT TO BE SARAH LUND

Let's get down to brass tacks. You like the smell of this adventure and you want in; but, to immerse yourself in the world of *Forbrydelsen* properly, you're going to need to emulate your heroine. Here are twenty simple exercises for you to try at home.

EXERCISE ONE

Stand, legs slightly akimbo, and stare off into the middle distance while imagining a gentle yet ominous tinkly piano playing a tune that says, 'Yes. I'm thinking now.'

If you can do this, then well done. You have taken your first steps to awesomeness. But let's not get giddy. There's a long way to go.

Sofie Says: '*I had no idea about the piano music in Series 1. When I was doing those scenes, I sometimes used to think about what was missing in my fridge.*'

✳︎ *Fun Fact:* When they shot the iconic *The Killing* poster picture for Series 1, Sofie had pulled the muscles in her neck and couldn't move her head. '*I hadn't slept all night*

1

and could literally not turn my head even the slightest to either side. Hence the paralysed, grave and very straight face.'

EXERCISE TWO

If you love *The Killing* or *Forbrydelsen*, as Danish people correctly call it, then you're already with me, wearing nothing but a pair of faded jeans, a jumper that may have been gifted by a distant, mildly eccentric aunt, and a pair of zip-up boots. By now, you should care for no other clothes. If, by a terrible twist of events, you still have any clothes other than the ones you're going to need then toss them into some boxes right now and send them to Sweden in a removal van. (But not *that* removal van, *that* wouldn't be appropriate.)

Sofie Says: 'It was brilliant that all her stuff was sent away in boxes. I felt wonderful about the fact that I was in the same outfit. I found it liberating. I hate changing my outfits. I hate it. With the costume you took away all the unrelated things. You make her sharp and simple.'

Fun Fact: For Series 3, they tried not giving Sarah Lund a jumper, but after two episodes they gave up and realized she needed one. She's also in heels during Episode 1 but after Sofie had to run in them and couldn't, they returned to the trusty boots.

Sofie Says: 'We couldn't escape having a jumper. Finding the jumper for the third series was traumatic. It took us ages to decide which one to have.' **Pssst:** You can see the Series 3 jumper towards the back of this book.

EXERCISE THREE

If you have long hair, tie it back. If you don't, grow it so you can. If you are a man then improvize by putting a lady's petticoat on your head and fastening it with an elastic band. It's a good look. Rock it.

Sofie Says: *'She ties her hair back when she's preparing to be professional. Loose hair softens her too much.'*

EXERCISE FOUR

Chew nicotine gum *endlessly*. You might want to try this . . .

Sofie Says: *'I chew nicotine gum in real life. Have done for twelve years. And when they stole this from me, I thought can't you come up with something on your own? And then I stopped and thought – hang on, nicotine gum is as expensive as cigarettes – they're going to give it to me for free. Joy.'*

EXERCISE FIVE

Someone's rung your mobile. Ascertain the facts and then hang up on them. *Never* say goodbye. Just *never*.

Sofie Says: *'What's so funny about this is that I had no idea I never said goodbye until you told me. You've spoilt it for me, Emma. I take a lot of calls in* The Killing *and sometimes I do say goodbye and when I do, I feel like I'm doing something wrong because you've told me she never says goodbye. To be honest, the police office is very low-tech. Sarah Lund can't even send a text.'*

✳ *Fun Fact:* Sofie actually regularly calls people by accident during scenes where she has to use the phone. *'I'm having to say my lines and I've got strangers going "Hello? Who is this? What are you talking about?"'*

EXERCISE SIX

Smiling is your mortal enemy. You are only allowed ten facial expressions from now on.

1. 'I am thinking now' face
2. 'As IF I fancy YOU' face
3. 'I am so right and you are so wrong' face
4. 'Oh shit, I'm not entirely sure how to shoot a gun' face
5. 'I couldn't give a toss what wood you want for the sauna' face
6. 'I hate people who eat Cheesy Wotsits in cars' face
7. 'My mother is talking to me but I'm not listening to a single thing she's saying' face
8. 'Please don't let that bloke I fancy be a psychopath' face
9. 'I will eat pizzas for clues' face
10. 'I am being told off by a superior but I'm going to do the exact opposite of what I'm being told' face

If you absolutely *have* to smile, make sure it's only at someone you think might have killed someone. Them's the rules. I don't make this shit up.

EXERCISE SEVEN

Someone is behaving in a manner that suggests they might be moving in for a kiss. Remain utterly, utterly motionless.

Stare at them as if you might club them over the head or buzz them with a cattle prod in the blink of an eye. It is very important to treat them with nothing but extreme suspicion.

(Trying to kiss Sarah Lund is like trout-tickling. It requires patience and skill and should only be undertaken by a professional. Do not attempt at home.)

Sofie Says: 'When it comes to romance, she just doesn't have the right frequency. To her, anyone giving off "I fancy you" vibes is like white noise. She's not tuned in.'

EXERCISE EIGHT
Only eat eggs whilst staring sadly out of the window. There are no exceptions to this rule. Stick to it.

Sofie Says: 'She does eat, but not much. Mainly, she only eats out of polystyrene or saucepans. That egg was her pushing the boat out cooking-wise. That's a posh dinner for her.'

EXERCISE NINE
If you're invited to a birthday party, don't sit down. Instead, stand in a doorway and casually scan the room for things that might give you ideas about clues. Parties and social gatherings are merely conduits to criminal case-cracking. They are *not* for socializing.

Nod at everyone, try and pretend you're happy, leave.

Sofie Says: 'I remember that scene clearly. She's such a misfit. When we filmed it there was a problem as there was

a small table and a lot of people so when everyone was
sitting down, I had to stand up and it felt really odd.'

EXERCISE TEN

Apply the same rule about birthday parties to weddings. It is absolutely crucial that you remain completely unmoved by emotional hoohah and stay focused on the higher things in life, like gruesome ritual killings.

If necessary, send yourself an unexplained bunch of flowers with a mysterious note and then use that as your flimsy excuse to get the hell out of there before the speeches start.

Sofie Says: 'She is phobic when it comes to social occasions. They're all singing a song and she wants to sing along but she hates trying. In Denmark we have a tradition where someone will take a well-known tune and rewrite the words to try and be funny. They rarely are, though. They're normally very badly written.'

EXERCISE ELEVEN

If someone you know tells you they're getting married in 48 hours, nod your head, pull your coat on and leave. Immediately.

Then forget they told you.

Then, when they remind you again, nod, pull your coat on and leave. Again.

Sofie Says: 'I completely forgot. Marriage is so unimportant, why would she be bothered to remember it? But I think she

really does make an effort. But she's just not able to be in
the world with other people and she's painfully aware of it.'

EXERCISE TWELVE

You've been told to bring a cake to a social gathering, but not
a cake that contains nuts because someone has a potentially
fatal nut allergy. It is, therefore, very, very important that
you don't forget about the nut thing.

Bring a cake that contains nuts.

Sofie Says: '*I know people like that, mostly men. They
really want to remember to bring the milk home for their
wife, but they're just not able to. That's who Sarah Lund is.*'

EXERCISE THIRTEEN

You've found yourself in a room with some people who may
or may not know something about a case. Don't bother
yourself with them. Stare at the photos on the walls instead.
Then, while they're burbling on, you can concentrate on
mustering a penetrating thought that goes straight to the
heart of the matter.

Do not blink during this exercise.

Sofie Says: '*Just wait for the piano tinkle . . . it will come.
She loves walking into rooms and staring. She's a nerd.*'

EXERCISE FOURTEEN

You're in a room with some walls. Lean against one of them
and fold your arms.

In an emergency situation, you may also stick your hands in your jean pockets and look awkward. (Also acceptable in this scenario.)

EXERCISE FIFTEEN
Never carry painkillers.

EXERCISE SIXTEEN
You're on the phone and being told that you absolutely must not go to a funeral to interview a severely bereaved man because a) he's suing the police for wrongful arrest, and b) he's severely bereaved.

Say nothing.

Instead, stare out of the window of your car and make a noise that means 'Wevers'.

Sofie Says: *'She has a strong sense of freedom and has a problem with authorities. She's in opposition to the system but she is the one who is going to save it.'*

EXERCISE SEVENTEEN
Only puke into buckets hanging off taps in boiler rooms.

Sofie Says: *'We had about half a minute to do that scene. I didn't have time to do it properly. It was one of the moments where I was inspired by men. Men and women puke differently. They have a different reaction to it. Women are embarrassed. Men aren't. So I decided to puke like a man.'*

EXERCISE EIGHTEEN

You've walked into a men's locker room where everyone is naked. Maintain eye contact at all times and remain unfazed, even in the presence of a very obvious and massive schlong.

Sofie Says: '*I was so looking forward to that scene. It was very nice. I've never done a scene like that before. I enjoyed it. It helped them a lot to be a bunch. That was fun.*'

EXERCISE NINETEEN

Someone in your family has asked you to help them prepare for their 'big day'. Give a non-committal reply, fail to turn up and have someone's coffin dug up instead.

Sofie Says: '*She didn't need me. She got everything done didn't she? Digging up a coffin is much more fun.*'

EXERCISE TWENTY

You've been taken off the case and asked to hand in your Police ID. Pay no attention. Instead, doggedly pursue trails of inquiry and if anyone asks any awkward questions such as 'Who you are and what's your authority?', simply wave your old business card in their face like a Jedi mind trick and plough on regardless.

You can fool everyone. *Everyone.*

(Except that woman who can lip-read. You can't fool her. Or that bloke at the baggage reclaim office. You can't fool him either. Actually, you can't fool anyone but don't let that stop you.)

Sofie Says: *'I love having a police badge. I love getting it out. But it's tricky. I have to practise ten times before I take it out because I'm always getting it out upside down.'*

Try and do these exercises for fifteen minutes every day. This is your baseline starting position on your journey to fabulousness.

So now let's make some deeper cuts. If you want to immerse yourself into the very being of Sarah Lund, you need to know every last thing about her. The following is your Fundamental (or Lundamental) Factsheet. Rip it out of the book and carry it with you at all times.

Height: 1 metre 69 cm

Weight: 57.2 kg

Boot Size: 36

Jumper Size: Small

Brand Of Jean: She never goes for brands. She's never had the same pair of jeans twice.

Handbag: Satchel. In it there is – lots of nicotine gum, keys, a flashlight, a pen and a pad.

Sofie Says: *'Confession: sometimes during interrogation scenes when lines were coming in very late, I wrote down my lines on that pad and then read them off it.'*

Model of gun: Heckler & Koch, USP Compact

Sofie Says: *'I hate that gun. I am hopeless. I have absolutely no idea what kind of gun it is. When men are wearing a gun they walk differently, like they just got off a horse. I didn't like wearing it as it makes her too self-assured. I was so bad at using it. In Series 1, in the blind woman's apartment, there's a dramatic close-up of Lund. I thought, oooh, this is like a real cop scene – the traditional shot where the gun is up in frame; and if you look, you'll see I've got two or three fingers in the trigger hole. There's only supposed to be one. They gave me shooting lessons but I was hopeless. To look good holding a gun it has to look like part of your body and it just didn't with me. I have short, fat fingers. I can't physically do it.'*

✳ Fun Fact: Søren Malling, who plays Jans Meyer in Series 1, also had shooting lessons with Sofie and he loved it so much he started clay-pigeon shooting. He's so good at it, he's now on the national team.

Beer: She takes any beer

Eggs: Fried

Sofie Says: *'Lund would never wait to boil an egg. If she tried to boil an egg it would have gone green before she got around to eating it. Forget about it.'*

University: Lund didn't go to university but did go to Police Academy. Not *that* Police Academy.

Sugar In Coffee? Strictly, she's a tea drinker. If she has to have a coffee it's with one sugar.

Awards: DAGA 4 and swimming certificates

You're now armed to the teeth with the ways of the Lund. Keep frowning. It's time to meet the rest of the gang.

2

SERIES ONE

Those Characters in Full

THE COLLEAGUES

....

✳ **Jans Meyer (Søren Malling)**
He's got ears like a toby jug and never goes anywhere without a banana but, mostly, he wants Lund to get the hell out of his office and leave for ever. Is there anything worse than being promoted and then having to lumber round after the person whose job you've taken while they quietly point out that every single idea you come up with is useless? No. Unless you count being killed, which, on the scale of rubbish things that can happen to you, is pretty high up.

He loves: Cheesy Wotsits and smoking
He hates: An acid stomach and anonymous flashlights
Most likely to say: 'Oh look, here's a plane ticket to Sweden, let me drive you to the airport.'
Forbrydelsen *Bingo Points:* He's in *Borgen*

Sofie Says: *'The chemistry between us was amazing. We were always giggling. Awful. In the scene where Lund is told that Bengt is in the hospital, we couldn't get through it. Ends of scenes where we had to stare at each other were always a problem too. Forever laughing. 'When I found out Meyer was going to die I cried and cried. It was ridiculous. When we got the script – Episode 18 – we read it and I was sitting opposite Søren. At the point where he's shot I got so sad. I loved that character. I could hardly read the lines. And I couldn't look at him because I knew I was going to cry. In the same room, at the side, there was like a changing area behind a curtain. When we finished the read-through I went in there, drew the curtain and tried to pull myself together. But Søren came in and the minute I saw him I broke down, then he broke down and we both had to cuddle each other. It's the only time I've ever cried at work.'*

Fun Fact: In the scene where he's shot, the fake blood they used was really sticky. Sofie ran at full speed towards Søren who was lying, wounded, on the floor, slipped in the blood and fell on top of his stomach, winding him really badly. Not only that, but the Effects Department had the blood pumping through a tube that had air in it, and as Sofie was trying to save Meyer's life the tube was making a farting noise.

Sofie Says: *'How we got through that scene I will never know.'*

Lovely Fact: Sofie and Søren have supper together every Sunday. Sofie now lives in the same block as Søren so they're neighbours.

❋ Lennart Brix (Morten Suurballe)

With the aura of a Bond villain's middle manager, Brix is Sarah Lund's boss. Like a spider, he only stands in the corners of rooms. Hands are kept in his pockets at all times. His hands. Not other people's. He has the permanent expression of someone who's forever wondering if he's left the iron on at home. He's a great fan of the man-scarf. Rumour has it Brix might be a vampire. Have you ever seen him in daylight? No. Neither have I.

He loves: The darkness of the night
He hates: Laughter, kittens and sun-filled meadows
Most likely to say: 'You're off the case'

Morten Says: 'On the question of whether I am a vampire, I can neither confirm nor deny.'

❋ *Fun Fact 1:* It was so cold during filming of Series 2 that Morten wore massive moonboots every time the shot was from the waist up.

❋ *Fun Fact 2:* Sofie thought Brix was the killer in Series 1.

Forbrydelsen *Bingo Points*: He's in *The Bridge*

❋ The Jumper

If it isn't a holy relic in Denmark already, it should be. Like another famous figure in history, Sarah Lund's jumper is sort of killed but then, miraculously, rises again three

days later without one single sign of damage. I am not saying Sarah Lund's jumper is the new Jesus. That can only be pronounced by a higher power than I. I am simply saying the facts speak for themselves. It died. It rose again. Let's leave it at that.

It loves: Invisible darning
It hates: Stabby men with knives
Most likely to say: 'Bow down before me mortals and quake!'

✳ **Fun Fact:** When Lund goes to Afghanistan in Series 2, she wears the jumper under her flak jacket; but it was so hot (they actually filmed it in Spain), she's only wearing the sleeves of the Jumper. Yes. I know. They *cut the Jumper up.*

✳ **Terrifying Fact:** When Sofie and Piv (the Producer) went to the Edinburgh TV Festival they entrusted the holy Jumper to Neil Midgeley, a freelance journalist. Neil, after *The Killing* session at the festival, put the Jumper into a plastic bag and then spent the rest of the day traipsing round Edinburgh with a friend. When he got back to his hotel he realized, with horror, that he was no longer carrying the bag. *He had lost the Jumper.* Thankfully, he retraced his steps the following day and tracked it down to a café in Jenners department store. A waitress had found the bag and bunged it in the staffroom. Neil *never* told Sofie or Piv. Pheee-ewwww.

✳ Buchard (Troels II Munk)
Lund's immediate boss. Despite having the aura of a kindly uncle, he's anything but. Shadowy forces in the upper eaves

of Police HQ are pulling this puppet's strings and forcing him to protect City Hall at all costs; but when it all collapses like a stack of dominoes made from rye bread, Buchard is the man who takes the fall, and in a strange packing boxes switcheroo, it's Lund's boss who ends up marching out of the job.

He loves: Deleting phone numbers from official evidence
He hates: Standing on his own at a leaving party wondering whether to wear a comedy Viking hat
Most likely to say: 'No. You're not going to Sweden.'

THE FAMILY

Nanna Birk Larsen (Julie R. Ølgaard)

The victim. Before coming to a ghastly and untimely end, Nanna was, according to all who knew her, a bit of a handful. She had a childhood sweetheart, an ex-boyfriend at school and a secret Proper Man lover who got her into all manner of trouble and turned out to be a right Moaning Minnie. All she wanted was to run off with a young man her parents didn't approve of and get married way too soon in a foreign country without any means of financially supporting herself. *What's wrong with that*? She has two brothers whom she calls the 'Teletubbies' but this is mostly because nobody in the Birk Larsen household knows what their real names are.

She loves: Amir and the Teletubbies
She hates: Being tied up in the boot of a car and dumped into a river
Most likely to say: 'I really wish I hadn't left my passport at that flat.'

✲ Theis Birk Larsen (Bjarne Henriksen)

The father of the deceased. Intense, brooding, like a dangerous bear, Theis is a man of few words, much given to sitting and staring out of his van drinking beer and pouting. He may have killed a man but nothing was proven. Even so, he doesn't shy from taking people to warehouses to beat the shit out of them. If he was a Superhero, he'd be called Captain Temper. You wouldn't want to cross him, especially if he's with Vagn and carrying a length of steel pipe.

He loves: Pernille and the 'boys'
He hates: Not wearing a bobble hat
Most likely to say: '...'

Bjarne Says: *'He's like a ticking bomb. He's walking round with all these muscles and he can't do a thing. Except beat up someone who had nothing to do with it. And be a bit scared of Pernille.'*

✲ ***Fun Fact:*** During a scene in Episode 1, Theis is with Vagn (Nicolaj Kopernikus) in the street in front of a grocer's stall. At the end of the scene, he takes an apple to eat it. During filming, as he went to eat it, the owner ran over to stop him because the apple was unsafe to eat.

Forbrydelsen *Bingo Points:* He's in *Borgen*

Sofie Says: *I went out for dinner with Bjarne once. We drank absinthe. I have never been so drunk in my life.*

✵ **Pernille Birk Larsen (Ann Eleonora Jørgensen)**
The mother of the deceased. Tortured with grief, she is the mistress of the despairing stare. Not only has her daughter been brutally murdered but she has to put up with her thick-set husband going vigilante on just about everybody who ever knew his daughter's ass. She's got enough on her plate without having to chase about town shouting 'THEIS!' every time he decides to maim someone. She's so distraught she can't actually remember what her sons are called other than 'the boys'.

She loves: Nanna, Theis and 'the boys'
She hates: The perpetrator
Most likely to say: 'Are you sure we didn't give them names?'

Ann Says: 'Was one of them called Jacob? Nickolej? No? I give up.'

✵ **Fun Fact 1:** Pernille never has a handbag for the entire series. Whenever she leaves the house, she takes nothing with her. Ann made a conscious decision to do this.

✳ **Fun Fact 2:** In the Birk Larsen apartment there's an aquarium. Every day, Ann would come in and feed the fish, thinking nobody else was doing so. But they were. One of the fish died. She fed it to death.

✳ **Fun Fact 3:** Sofie has some furniture from the Birk Larsen apartment in her own flat. She took a few of the lamps and the Jacobsen chairs.

✳ The Boys Birk Larsen: (Jonas Leth Hansen and Kasper Leth Hansen)

So rarely are they called by their actual names you'd be forgiven for thinking they have no names at all other than 'the boys' or 'the Teletubbies'. Never allowed to take their coats off, the boys spend most of their time hoping they're going to fly a kite or have a go on a remote-controlled car only to have every dream they've ever had smashed to smithereens. They also go down in history as having the worst birthday party ever.

They love: Flying kites and dressing up in their scout uniforms

They hate: That dog and never getting to go anywhere

Most likely to say: 'Oh look, here's the blood-splattered passport of my sister who was just murdered. I'll just leave it under this cupboard and not mention it to my parents. That'll teach them never to call me by my own name.'

Bjarne Says: *'I have absolutely no idea what they were called.'*

✳ **Vagn Skaerbaek (Nicolaj Kopernicus)**
Devoted to Theis and Pernille. And not in a good way. Unless you think brutally raping their daughter repeatedly over multiple locations and then drowning her by driving a car into a river is the best way he could have come up with to convey that devotion. I dunno. I'd have been happy with giving them chocolates or something, or maybe fixing some shelves. He's killed before, has a penchant for necklaces and is blessed with the greatest 'I Am The Killer' face in television history. This is unfortunate given that everyone watched Episode 1, shouted 'It's him! It's him!' every time his sneaky face popped up and then had to convince themselves that it couldn't possibly be that obvious for the next 19 episodes.

He loves: Killing young women he's stared at for years
He hates: Himself
Most likely to say: 'Oh come on! I only killed your daughter! Can't we just forget about it and move on? I want to take the boys out! You know? The boys?'

Nicolaj Says: *'I wore the hat for a reason. I was going to be filming* The Killing *for almost two years and I wanted to be able to do other jobs at the same time; I figured if I wore a hat then I could change my hair for other roles.'*

✳ ***Fun Fact 1:*** When they were filming Episode 2, a fax

arrived at the production office saying Vagn was the killer. Nicolaj saw it by accident but the next day was told to 'Forget it', so from then on, every scene they filmed he did one version in which he thought 'I am the killer' and then another version in which he thought 'No, I'm not.'

❋ **Fun Fact 2:** In Denmark, Nicolaj is best known for warm, comic roles so it was a big shock for him to be the Prince of Darkness in *The Killing*.

Forbrydelsen *Bingo Points*: He's in *The Bridge*.

❋ Charlotte (Laura Drasbæk)

The slightly racy younger sister of Pernille who thinks the best advice to give a niece is to go and work in a sleazy club called Boils, pick up an older man and then rattle onwards on a train track to disaster. She's the worst aunt *ever*. Not only that, but she's clearly not blessed in the brains department given that it takes her almost a fortnight to actually remember that Nanna used to work with her and had a boyfriend who may or may not have killed her.

She loves: Working at Boils
She hates: Having to remember stuff. It's just so thinky.
Most likely to say: 'Wow. Those boots are revolting.'

CITY HALL

✵ Troels Hartmann (Lars Mikkelsen)

The man who never blinks. Troels (TROOOOOOOOELLLLLLS) is determined to take the top job at City Hall, Troels (TROOOOOOOOEELLLLLLLLLLLS) is hell bent on doing everything he can to take political pedantry to new levels. There's not a sub-clause on Procedural Propriety he doesn't know about. Having said that, he did call himself Faust on a dating website, tried to kill himself in a log cabin and gave his opponent a heart attack, so he's not all good.

He loves: Democracy, rubbish collection in Ørestad, refurbishing city sports facilities and Appendix 13X
He hates: The Mayor
Most likely to say: 'Call a press conference, I'm challenging the Mayor to a Staring Contest.'

Lars Says: *'I based the character of Troels on a politician who used to be an actor. He's not a politician any more. He was a better actor, to be honest.'*

✵ ***Fun Fact:*** The costume department had to widen Lars's trousers because, after he gave up smoking, he put on 10 kilos. (He smokes again now.)

Forbrydelsen *Bingo Points:* He's in *Those That Kill*

❋ Morten Weber (Michael Moritzen)

What's a geography teacher doing at City Hall? That's no geography teacher. That's the evillest mind the civil service in Denmark has ever seen. He's also the thickest. (Please see 'Those Pesky Plot Holes'.) The man is an idiot. Despite this, he's managed to secure himself firmly at the right-hand side of Troels (TROOOO- OOOELLLLLS), where he's got passing pieces of paper in an urgent fashion down to a fine art.

He loves: Troels (TROOOOOOOOELLLLLS), shoes with special cushioning and Egyptian foot cream
He hates: Blood-stained flats and yeasty buns
Most likely to say: 'If I just give this stairwell a wipedown nobody will ever notice.'

❋ Rie Skovgaard (Marie Askehave)

Watch out. Vamp alert. She's the va-va-voom of City Hall, the attractive one we must automatically be suspicious of. She can't bear Sarah Lund, mostly because she doesn't wear lipstick but also because she keeps turning up at City Hall trying to arrest her boyfriend. The lipstick thing annoys her more, though.

She loves: Troels (Troooooellllls)
She hates: Sarah Lund
Most likely to say: 'Hello, is that the Chief of Police? Can you sack Sarah Lund now please? Thanks so very.'

Marie Says: *'I had a kissing scene with Lars and between takes I could smell meatballs. And I said "What's that smell?" And Lars said, "That's me. I just farted."'*

✳ **Fun Fact 1:** Marie's mother is an extra in Episode 9

✳ **Fun Fact 2:** The actress who plays Rie's replacement in Episode 20 used to go out with Marie's husband. Not only that, but the same actress is married to Jens Holck in real life.

Forbrydelsen *Bingo Points*: She's in *Borgen* Series 3

✳ **Jens Holck (Jesper Lohmann)**
Beware the quiet ones. That's what my mother told me. Who'd a-thunk it eh? Jens Holck, the man who looks as if he's never happier than in a potting shed. The man who gives off the whiff of a toasty cardigan. The man who you'd never guess in a million years was cheating on his wife with a teenage girl and then, when said teenage girl was done with him, would turn into a weirdybonk stalker, kill a man for no sensible reason and then go crack-a-lack mental, take Sarah Lund hostage, scrape the blessed Jumper across an oily floor with not one thought for it and who then, instead of killing Lund when he has the chance, botches it and ends up dead himself. What a twat.

He loves: Nanna Birk Larsen and going to Latvia
He hates: New boyfriends and snitches
Most likely to say: 'Pleeeeease will you still go out with me? Pleeeeeeeeeease?'

Forbrydelsen *Bingo Points:* He's in *Borgen*

✳ Mayor Poul Bremer (Bent Mejding)

Like a game-show host from the mid seventies, Mayor Bremer is far too jolly to be in charge of anything other than commentating on grown adults dressed in oversized rubber outfits trying to negotiate water obstacles. He never stops smiling. Ever. You might think this is so he can keep his friends close and his enemies closer but it's not. It's because he suffers from terrible wind.

He loves: A mint after a testy TV debate
He hates: Pernickety rules
Most likely to say: 'Chest pain! CHEST PAIN!'

THE LUND FAMILY

✳ Vibeke Lund (Anne Marie Helger)

The term 'long-suffering' springs to mind. Sarah Lund's mother has been rolling her eyes at her daughter since time began. Her daughter doesn't eat properly, doesn't look after her son properly, doesn't do what her boyfriend wants properly and is utterly hopeless at sitting still, listening to speeches at weddings or staying for any sort of cake at any family-shaped celebration. Why oh why did she let Sarah go into the police force? She could have pickled herrings for a living. Or made jumpers. But oh no, she had to go off and become a one-woman crime-fighting unit without a second thought for anyone around her. And don't get her started on Sarah's relationships. One failed marriage tucked under her belt, she finally gets someone to go out with her and what does she do? Packs her stuff off to Sweden and then doesn't bother to go. Well screw her. She's made her bed and she can lie in it.

She loves: Tutting and looking disappointed
She hates: Endlessly picking up Sarah's pants from the flat floor
Most likely to say: 'I don't mean to be funny but that jumper's starting to whiff.'

✳ **Fun Fact:** She's a comedian and has her own show in Denmark. She's also politically very active.

⋮ **Sofie Says:** *'We were shooting at City Hall and outside there was a demonstration that was really loud and mucking up the sound. Suddenly Anne Marie's voice piped up - she was talking through a loudhailer at the demo!'*

✳ **Mark (Eske Forsting Hansen)**
Mark, Sarah Lund's son, spends most of his time staring out of the car window quietly fretting that his mother has no interest in him whatsoever. And he'd be right. It's a miracle she even remembers his name. She doesn't even know what size jumper he wears, for crying out loud. Thank goodness his dad's a sensible spectacle-wearing type of guy with a penchant for a man-scarf.

He loves: Listening to songs about depression and not pulling his trousers up properly
He hates: Sweden and everything it stands for
Most likely to say: 'No. I don't think my mum will be doing the egg and spoon race. No.'

Sofie Says: '*He's grown up on the show. In the first series he was in his early teens and he found it quite hard staying awake early in the morning. In the scene where we're driving to the airport, Anne Marie had to keep elbowing him awake.*'

✳ Bengt Rosling (Johan Gry)

Right. So let's state one thing from the off. Sarah Lund's boyfriend is a Criminal Profiler and he wonders what Sarah Lund sees in him. Yeah. Right. All those nights whispering sweet nothings while Sarah stares at the ceiling and says things like, 'White male? 30–40? Will kill again?' This is the equivalent of any other woman marrying a man who owns a handbag factory. We know it's all over when Bengt starts wanging on about what wood she might want in the sauna. *She doesn't care.* She's not interested in your interior design angst. She just wants the lowdown on unsolved murders. That's it. Coincidence she chucks him the *minute* he's looked at that mysterious file? *I think not.*

He loves: Sarah Lund and saunas
He hates: The wrong type of wood
Most likely to say: 'I don't know. Pine gives you odour but larch gives you depth.'

THOSE MINOR CHARACTERS IN FULL

....

✳ Oliver Schandorff (Cyron Bjørn Melville)

Nanna's ex-boyfriend. Suspect number two. With the normal aura of a half-washed, hormonal teenager, Oliver spends much of his time having sex or thinking about when he's going to have more sex.

He likes: When his parents go away for the weekend
He hates: When chicks' dads come round and storm up your stairs demanding to know if you've just boned their daughter
Most likely to say: 'Hello. I'm Oliver. Can we have sex now?'

✳ Jeppe Hald (Casper Steffensen)

President of the Student Council and suspect number three. Your classic mucky pup, he's grubby in a way that only a young man can be. Already predisposed to making sex tapes, Jeppe is set to go far.

He likes: Sex and lots of it
He hates: When your sex tapes get out
Most likely to say: 'No, we don't need to see your face.'

✳ Lisa (Laura Christensen)

Nanna's best friend. Or so she says. BFFs tell each other everything. That's basic. But Lisa knows pretty much zip about Nanna's personal life outside of the school walls, which makes her the most useless best friend since Judas.

She likes: Threesomes in basements whilst wearing a witch's hat

She hates: Awkward questions about threesomes in basements
Most likely to say: 'How come I'm the only one having to wear a costume?'

✲ John Lynge (Benjamin Boe Rasmussen)

Suspect number one. He's the temp hired by the Volunteers' Office. He's also a known criminal with a penchant for preying on old blind ladies and their cats, he has no respect for holy Jumpers and he'll leap out of a window at a moment's notice. To conclude: volatile.

He likes: Cats
He hates: Coming down with norovirus while delivering posters
Most likely to say: 'Hang on a minute . . . didn't I leave a car here?'

✲ Rahman Al Kemal (Farshad Kholghi)

He's the Danish teacher at Frederiksholm School, a city Role Model, a secret helper of young illegal immigrants, a dad-to-be and a lover of model helicopters. He's also not half bad at basketball. That to one side, he's still suspect number five, which is bad luck on him.

He likes: The novels of Karen Blixen
He hates: Finding himself in the back of a van with a lot of explaining to do
Most likely to say: 'So I'm at your house. You think I killed your daughter. Gosh. This is awkward.'

✳ Olav Christensen (Kristian Ibler)

Olav, or 'Chippy Miller', as his pals call him, is the slightly tetchy civil servant hell-bent on exacting a quiet revenge on Troels. He hides files down the backs of cupboards, he lets any old flibbertigibbet have the keys to the Party flat and he accepts backhanders as if they were going out of fashion. What a shame, then, that he didn't take the time to learn his Green Cross Code.

He likes: The sweet smell of promotion
He hates: Troels and the unnerving sense of a noose tightening
Most likely to say: 'Green man's flashing! Green man's fla....aaaaaaarrrggggh.'

✳ Leon Frevert (Peder Holm Johansen)

Oh Leon, with your suspicious face and the seam of terror running through your very core. He's the taxi driver who picks up Nanna and takes her to 130 Store Kongensgade and so sets in motion the chain of events that leads to her grisly death. If only he'd kept his gob shut the whole awful mess might never have happened. Having said that, if he hadn't flapped his trap then we wouldn't have Sarah Lund so, you know, swings and roundabouts.

He likes: Tittle-tattling
He hates: Eye contact with detectives
Most likely to say: 'Honest Vagn, I won't tell *anyone*.'
Forbrydelsen *Bingo Points*: He's in *The Bridge*

✳ Nethe Stjernfeldt (Maibritt Saerens)

This saucy minx, otherwise known by her online persona, 'Fanny Hill', is the woman who nails Troels in more ways than one. Not only that, but she's the only person who *sees* the Killer in situ at the Party flat. If only she had better eyesight.

She likes: Online dating and all the illicit encounters it brings
She hates: Being asked awkward questions within earshot of her blissfully ignorant husband
Most likely to say: 'I'll be the one wearing the red carnation.'

✳ Phillip Dessau (Jakob Cedergren)

He's only got a fleeting role but it's a crucial one. He's fallen charm to Rie's hypnotic ways and, like so many men before him, has let slip political secrets in exchange for a grubby rub. And who can blame him?

He likes: Below-board meetings in hotel rooms that involve alcohol and very few clothes
He hates: Unedifying shoving scenes at the bottom of long staircases
Most likely to say: 'I thought you were going to bin him? *Jesus*!'

Marie Says: 'Rie tells Troels that she didn't sleep with Phillip Dessau. But she did. And then, she did it again.'

✳ Amir El Namen (Omar Kamounah)

Nanna's own true love. If only he'd alerted Theis or Pernille or the police on Friday night when Nanna failed to turn up. If only he'd done that. If only Nanna had been a lesbian. A woman would have called the police after one text message had gone unanswered. Tops.

He loves: Nanna and romantic notions

He hates: Sitting on bridges staring down into a river of misery

Most likely to say: 'I would have called the police but my battery ran out. And I didn't know the number. If you can think of any other excuses, feel free to pass them on.'

And finally . . .

✳ The Policeman With No Name (Ole Boison)
Now then, this is an exclusive. Remember this guy? He's the one Lund pulls the gun on in Episode 20. Well – guess what – this is the guy who is watching Lund and is feeding back all the info on the case to Rie. Yes. I know. *That* nutty hangonaminute is now finally answered. Ithankyow.

Forbrydelsen *Bingo Points*: He's in *The Bridge*

✳ *Scary Fact:* In Series 1 the set for the Police HQ was quite small and the ceiling was made from a type of compressed paper that dulls echoes and is best for sound. One day in August, they were filming and Sofie says she had never been so hot. Suddenly a filter caught fire, they were all evacuated and the fire brigade were called. They took the temperature. On the floor it was 45 degrees and on the ceiling it was 72 degrees. *'We're lucky we didn't all go up in smoke.'* The set had to be shut down and the Police HQ rebuilt.

Now let's crack on with more unexplained stuff . . .

Those Pesky Plot Holes

Sometimes, in any long-running murder mystery hoohah, some things are simply never explained. But I am ready to shine the torch of truth into dark corners. It is now time for us to don the cloak of doubt and penetrate those unanswered questions that left us hanging like a mountaineer without a rope.

BEWARE: THE FOLLOWING IS SO FULL OF SPOILERS YOU SHOULD ONLY READ THIS BIT IF YOU HAVE SEEN BOTH SERIES. I AM PROPERLY WARNING YOU. DON'T COME CRYING IF EVERYTHING IS RUINED.

Fun Fact: *Forbrydelsen* was originally called *Historien om et mord* ('The Story of a Murder') but they wanted to change the title to *Drabet* ('The Killing'). However, a Danish film came out called *Drabet* so, instead, they called it *Forbrydelsen*, which actually means 'The Crime'. Yes. We're all calling it the wrong name. Suck on that.

THE PLOT

The body of Nanna Birk Larsen has been found in the boot of a car at the bottom of a lake. Sarah Lund, detective extraordinaire, is on her last day at work. She's off to Sweden to live with her Criminal Profiler boyfriend Bengt Rosling. All her things are packed up but Sarah is told she can't leave until the case is solved, much to the chagrin of the detective due to take over from her, Jan Meyer. They need to work together in order to chase down a ruthless killer. At City Hall, mayoral elections are under way, and as evidence drags local politician Troels Hartmann into the investigation, political intrigue becomes interwoven with an ever-changing case.

OK. So that's all very well, but there are more twists and turns in Series 1 than in a lower intestine. So here, for your simple pleasure, is the timeline of who was what, where, how and with whom.

Nanna Birk Larsen was planning to run away with her childhood sweetheart, Amir El Namen. She attended a party at her school but left early. She went to her school teacher's house by bike to return some books and then, finding her bike stolen, she got a cab, driven by Leon Frevert, to 130 Store Kongensgade where she met Jens Holck. She needed to go into the flat to retrieve her passport. The passport was there because she went to Paris with Jens and left her passport in the flat.

Earlier that evening, Troels Hartmann had been at the flat getting drunk because it was the anniversary of his wife's death. She had cancer but had refused treatment because she was pregnant. He decides to kill himself in his wife's old summer house. He has driven to the flat in the campaign car but gets a cab to the summer house. He then tries to gas himself but fails to do so because a door blows open.

Meanwhile, Leon has rung Theis but gets Vagn instead. Leon tells him that Nanna is planning to run away. Vagn then goes to the flat to try and stop Nanna but instead ends up raping her. Vagn then takes the car keys to the campaign car which have been left by Troels earlier and drives Nanna to Theis's new house, where he keeps her in the basement. He rapes her again.

The following morning, Morten goes to the Party flat and discovers the grisly scene. He cleans blood from the door and stairs and refuses to let in a workman who has arrived to fit a new toilet. He then goes to the summer house, where he finds Troels.

Rie, Troels's girlfriend, upset that she doesn't know where Troels is, has spent Friday night with Phillip Dessau. She goes to the conference centre on her own the following morning and conducts meetings without Troels.

Vagn takes Nanna to the woods. She escapes but he captures her. Very early on Sunday morning, he puts her into the boot of the campaign car and drives it into the river. She drowns.

Nanna's body is discovered on Monday evening.

OK. So now let's look at the line-up of suspects in the order they come rolling in.

SUSPECT 1: JOHN LYNGE

A temp hired by the Volunteers' Office from time to time. He's a known criminal. He drove the campaign car from City Hall to Nanna's school to deliver posters. While there he fell ill and went to the hospital. He left the keys to the campaign car in the ignition.

Other notable deeds: he holds a blind woman captive and he slashes the Jumper. Rather than be caught, he leaps from a window and sustains multiple fractures. While in hospital, he identifies our next suspect.

SUSPECTS 2 & 3: JEPPE HALD & OLIVER SCHANDORFF

A tape comes to light in which a woman, wearing Nanna's witch's hat from the party, is having sex with Oliver, Nanna's ex-boyfriend, and Jeppe, the president of the Student Council, in a secret room in the basement of the school. It's not Nanna. It's Lisa. And the reason for the blood is because she broke a glass and she fell over into it.

SUSPECT 4: HENNING KOFOED

Teacher at Nanna's school writing a paper on trends in language. He has an essay written by Nanna about a young girl who has an affair with an older man. It's described as 'intense'. He has some dodgy pornographic magazines in his flat, but he's not our guy. Instead he points the finger at . . .

SUSPECT 5: RAHMAN AL KEMAL

Rahman gets himself into all manner of difficulties because he refuses to come clean as to where he was at the time of Nanna's disappearance. Matters aren't helped by the fact that Nanna came to see him, nor by the fact that a neighbour sees him and an accomplice carrying a body into the back of a van. Things take a turn for the worse after the discovery of a garage with a mattress in it and a bloody yellow top which may have belonged to Nanna.

But he's not our guy. He was helping a young Muslim girl, Leyla Jamal, who has run away to avoid an arranged marriage. He is only cleared after they find his accomplice, Mustafa Akkad, who confirms Rahman's alibi.

SUSPECT 6: THE SECURITY GUY AT CITY HALL

This dear old fellah just happened to be passing Nanna's school. He sees the campaign car with the keys in it and decides to drive it back to the City Hall car park. He fills it up with petrol on the way back.

So *who* took the car from the City Hall car park? The surveillance tape that could shed light on this has gone missing. It's been stolen by Morten Weber. But grainy CCTV footage emerges which gives us our next guy.

SUSPECT 7: TROELS HARTMANN

Lund has discovered the bloody hell in the Party flat. What's more, Nanna Birk Larsen had keys to the flat. Troels refuses to come clean as to where he was on the night of the murder; there's a murky trail of paper that suggests he's been paying off dodgy civil servant Olav Christensen and a revelation that he is Faust, the online dating profile who has been emailing Nanna Birk Larsen. He's charged with the murder. But he's not our guy . . .

Someone texted Nanna repeatedly from a City Hall trip to Latvia. And someone in a white station wagon has killed Olav Christensen. Which leads Lund to suspect:

SUSPECT 8: PHILLIP DESSAU

He's Mayor Bremer's advisor and was on the trip to Latvia. A call is put out to find his white car. But when it's found, there's not a scratch on it. He's not our guy.

So Lund goes off to have a chat with someone else who was on the Latvia trip . . .

SUSPECT 9: JENS HOLCK

Lund finds the white station wagon that was used to kill Olav. Jens was having an affair with Nanna Birk Larsen. He was using the Party flat without Troels's knowledge, and was paying Olav Christensen to arrange the bookings. One night, at the flat, he found Troels's laptop. Troels had left the Boils dating website up and was still logged in so Jens used his Faust profile to contact Nanna. They had an affair but Nanna broke it off. On the night Nanna was abducted, he met her at the flat. He then went and waited at the airport to try and stop her leaving.

He didn't kill her. But he did kill Olav Christensen, who was about to spill the beans about the bookings.

Jens has clearly lost his tiny mind. But he's not our guy . . .

So now Lund is at a dead end. She turns her mind to that file of unsolved murders and finds the file on Mette Hauge. She discovers that Mette had the same necklace as was found in the fist of Nanna Birk Larsen. There is also a connection to a removal firm, Merkur – and guess who used to work for them . . .

SUSPECT 10: VAGN SKAERBAEK

But he was at a nursing home on the night Nanna was abducted wasn't he? He was for a bit, and then he left. But before Lund can get to the bottom of the Vagn connection she also discovers that Nanna was planning to run away with Amir. She finds him and he tells her that someone wearing a Birk Larsen uniform saw them that night. Again the finger points to Vagn, but Amir fails to identify him in a line-up. Lund goes to check out Vagn's flat but a chance encounter and an unexpected chase leads us to . . .

SUSPECT 11: LEON FREVERT

He was the taxi driver who picked Nanna up on the night she was abducted. He knows that Vagn went to the Party flat to sort her out and is running scared. He takes off, hoping to escape, but is tracked down by Vagn, who kills him and makes it look like suicide.

And everyone thinks the case is over. But it's not. Lund goes to check an old storage unit rented by Mette's father but when she gets there someone else has beaten her to it, broken in and stolen a photograph from an album. The perpetrator is in the building at the same time as Lund and Meyer and, trying to escape, he shoots Meyer.

Before Meyer dies, he keeps repeating one thing over and over – 'Sara 84'. Lund goes to Theis's new house to ask Vagn some questions about Leon. As they are leaving Vagn puts on a top, on the front of which is stitched 'SARAJEVO 84'.

Which gives us . . .

SUSPECT 10 (again): VAGN SKAERBAEK

And he's the one who did it.

✳ *Sad Fact:* A family in Denmark contacted Sofie because their mother, who was dying of cancer, was worried she was going to die before the identity of the killer was revealed.

Sofie Says: 'I sent her two envelopes. One was a letter and the other had the plot explanation in it. When she knew she was going to die, she opened it but then tore it to pieces and taped the pieces up so that nobody would be able to see it. She's the only person I've ever told who the killer was.'

Questions, Questions, So Many Questions

Fine, that's that explained; but there are many other questions. So many other questions. So come with me now through my Curtain of Unravelling Mysteries and all will be revealed . . .

OK. So in Series 1 we've got 20 episodes. It's hard to keep up and keep track, and there were more red herrings than a convention for red herrings in a conference centre made of herrings all of which are red.

At the beginning, where is Lund going?
She's moving to Sweden to live with her boyfriend Bengt Rosling. They're going to live in Sigtuna, which is quite remote.

Why is it so very dark?
Denmark has the highest investment in wind turbines in Europe. Electricity is expensive. Therefore, nobody turns their lights on. Q.E.D.

The Killing is always set in November. It gets dark at 3.30 p.m. The sun rises around 8.30 so they have very few hours of sunlight.

Sofie Says (cheekily): *'It's the human darkness as well, Emma.'*

What does Troels mean when he says 'I don't read books with orange covers'?
It's a joke. He's referring to a Cicero book Bremer is telling him to read – subtext is 'I don't read your books, I couldn't care less.'

Lars Says: *'This was an improvised moment. I wanted to convey the sense that Troels would never take anything from Bremer. But books with orange covers aren't a 'thing' in Denmark. There's no particular significance in that.'*

Theis shows Vagn the new house for the first time halfway through Episode 1. But Vagn has already taken Nanna there over the weekend. How did he know about it? And how did he have a key?

Nicolaj Says: *'He's Theis's best friend – he's always round their stuff. He knows Theis has bought a house. He also knows it's empty and that Theis is away for the weekend so nobody is going to turn up. When we shot that scene I had no idea I was the killer, but because I was given the plaster to wear on my neck I wondered if I might be. So I played this scene as if Vagn is slightly on edge but not too much so that it would not be obvious.'*

✳ ***Fun Fact:*** Because Nicolaj always had it in his mind that he might be the killer, when they came to film the funeral scene, he did one version in which he was weeping and another where he was ice-cold.

Nicolaj Says: *'I imagined, as a character trait, that Vagn was a poker player. I used to walk around with poker chips in my pockets. He's a risk-taker. He has a dual life.'*

When did Vagn do the flooring in the basement to cover up the blood? Wasn't he busy in the forest killing Nanna all weekend?

He meets Nanna at the flat on Friday evening and takes her to the basement later that night. He keeps her in the basement all of Saturday and then, very early on Sunday morning, he takes her to the woods. When you see her running away in the opening credits, it's about 6 a.m. on Sunday morning. Vagn spends all of Sunday fixing the floor.

Why did he take her to the forest? Why didn't he finish her off at the flat or the house?
It would be easier to dispose of the body in the forest. Also, Vagn tells Theis at the end that he couldn't physically kill Nanna. This is why he puts her in the boot of the car and drives it into the river.

Plus, he's a maniacal serial killer. They do this shit.

𝒩icolaj Says: '*By doing that he's absolving himself of responsibility. It's as if he didn't actually kill her. When he tells Theis this, it's as close as he's going to get to saying sorry.*'

What is the make of car Nanna is found in?
It's a Ford Mondeo station car.

We've got 19 episodes to go and Pernille and Theis have got to be miserable from here on. That's a tough gig isn't it?
You betcha. Miserable as hell for almost two years. Day in. Day out. It's like working in a pet crematorium.

Ann Says: '*This was a really hard balance. Give too much too soon and people will be bored. Give too little and nobody will care. Pernille only cries once, at the end of Episode 1, and that's it. From then on she's holding it all in but the grief is with her always. The clothes helped a* lot. I picked that trenchcoat and wouldn't let them put me in anything else. This is a woman who has stopped caring what she looks like. She wants to be plain, drab. But it did get to the stage where I thought, Pernille needs to kill someone now. It's a shame she didn't get to.'

✳ **Fun Fact:** When Series 1 was on, wherever Ann went, people wanted to hug her. *'I was in the UK trying to buy some wrinkle cream and a woman wouldn't let go of me.'*

So where did Nanna go after the party? I'm confused.

Nanna leaves the school on her bike and cycles to Rahman's house to return the two Karen Blixen books he had lent her. When she comes out, she discovers her bike has been stolen so she hails down a cab. The cab is driven by Leon. He drops her off at 130 Store Kongensgade, the Party flat. She has to go there to meet Jens to get the keys to the flat so she can let herself in and find her passport

What was Nanna's passport doing in the flat?

She left it there during a saucy assignation with Jens Holck. The minx.

But why did she take her passport to the flat? What teenager carries around their passport?

She went to Paris with Jens and left her passport at the flat. She's a teenager. They have the memories of peas.

So Lisa, Nanna's best friend, didn't know about Jens Holck or Amir? Really?

No. She really didn't. Nanna was a woman of mystery.

Who gave Troels's diary to the journalist? In fact, who is leaking all the information on Troels?
We're meant to think it's Morten as the emails came from his computer. But he couldn't have sent them because he was outside meditating. It was Olav Christensen, who hates Troels's guts.

Sorry? Morten meditates?
Yes. I know.

How did Troels get to the summer house?
He took a cab. He was shit-faced on brandy. He'd had the best part of a bottle. How he didn't hurl his guts all over the taxi I shall never know.

So whose car was seen in the driveway?
Morten's. He went there on Saturday to look for Troels.

The log cabin in which Troels tries to kill himself seems quite sturdy. Yet as he lies, head in oven, the door blows open, thus saving his life. How can this be? That log cabin looked extremely well constructed?
It was a very windy night. The end.

Lars Says: *'I don't think he really did want to commit suicide. It's his Hamlet moment. He's visited by the ghost of his dead wife, who saves him. A ghost that can open heavy wooden doors, obviously.'*

When did Morten go to the flat and why didn't he report it?
He went there on Saturday morning. He didn't report it because he's been waiting 12 years for political change and

he didn't want to jeopardize the election so he was going to wait till after the election to tell anyone.

Also, he's an idiot.

You've got to be kidding me?
That's what the man said.

But hang on. If Morten went there on Saturday then he didn't know Nanna had been murdered. But after it's revealed a girl is dead, he still doesn't say anything? What's the matter with him? It might have been Troels!
I refer you to my previous statement. The man is an idiot.

Lars Says: 'Morten is in love with Troels. He will do anything to protect him. I'm not sure it's sexual but this job is his life and he will do anything to preserve it.'

How did Morten manage to go to the flat, clean the stairs and handles, flush the sponges down the toilet and leave not one trace of his own DNA anywhere?
There would have been DNA of him in the flat. But that wouldn't have been abnormal. He gets to use it all the time. It's not an issue.

How come Vagn goes to the trouble of cleaning Nanna's nails so there's no DNA but leaves the flat in such a terrible state?
It's an act of love for Nanna. This is why he cleans her body and bathes her – it has nothing to do with trying to cover his tracks.

Also, Vagn didn't have a key to the flat so couldn't get back in to clean up; but the flat has no association with him so it conveniently frames other people. It makes sense to leave it in a state. But it was primarily a question of time. Vagn doesn't know how long they'll remain undisturbed. He has to move her quickly.

The basement, on the other hand, would have to be cleaned because Theis would see it and Vagn would therefore be an immediate suspect.

How come Vagn left no DNA in the flat? Why was this never investigated?
The forensic scientists were having a very bad few days at work. We've all done it.

: *Sofie Says:* '*He was wearing a really tight latex body suit. Obviously.'** (AUTHOR'S NOTE: I think Sofie Gräbøl might be fibbing.)

So we're meant to believe that Vagn simply wanted to stop Nanna leaving the country. But then it all went tits up and he ended up raping her and killing her? Really? So was it an accident? Or did he take her leaving as his chance to kill her after all those years of wanting to?
I think we can all state once and for all that, yes, Vagn may have over-reacted.

Nicolaj Says: '*The minute she's raped it's all over. She's the only girl on earth he can talk to. He has seen her naked and growing up. He was part of the furniture. He's picked her up from parties. So close to her. He crossed a borderline. He's filled with sexual energy brought on by jealousy because she's running away. And once he starts, he can't stop.*'

Why did no one else in the block of flats notice the blood on the stairs? Or hear the inevitable racket that must have come from the apartment when Nanna was being attacked?

The other apartments are businesses and the block is always empty at the weekends. Plus, Morten went over the banisters with a wet sponge.

Explain to me what's going on when Leon happily tells the police he picked Nanna up as if he doesn't know her? He works for Theis! Of course he knows her!

He did recognize her. His first story to the police is bogus. He's told to tell the police this story by Vagn. So yes, they did chat and Nanna told him she was leaving to go away with Amir and that's what Leon told Vagn. If Leon hadn't told Vagn, Nanna would still be alive.

Did Leon know Vagn killed Nanna? And if yes, why didn't he say something?

He doesn't know for definite. He knows Vagn went to the Party flat that night but that's it. He becomes obsessed with the case, more from fear for his own safety than anything else, and this explains the cuttings on his walls when Lund finds his flat. He's trying to work it out.

So what is the best wood to use in a sauna?

Polar pine. It's better than ordinary pine because it has less resin. You're welcome.

Sofie Says: 'Classic example of sexes being reversed – like a woman phoning her husband to ask what tiles he wants in the bathroom. Lund couldn't care less what wood is in the

: sauna. *In fact, I can't even imagine Lund in a sauna. I don't*
: *know what she was thinking.'*

Why doesn't anyone turn the lights on when they go into Mrs Heiberg's flat?

The Danish abhor an overhead light.

: **Sofie Says:** *'We were being very quiet when we entered*
: *but I was glad it was dark because I was so bad at holding*
: *the gun. And anyway, Mrs Heiberg doesn't need lights. She's*
: *blind.'*

When the Jumper gets slashed to bits by John Lynge, how come there's no sign of darning or fixing when it makes its triumphant return?

I think we can assume that the Jumper (*genuflects*) is mended by Vibeke, Sarah's mother, who is obviously a seamstress of some sort. We see her making a wedding dress at one point so she must be a whizz at stitching.

Who withheld Rahman's file from Troels and the police?

It was Olav Christensen. Again. The man's a nuisance.

Why does he hate Troels so much and who is he working for?

Troels turned him down for promotion two years ago. Olav thinks he's working for Bremer. But he's not. He's a mere pawn in Jens Holck's grand scheme.

What is Pernille's tattoo?

We only see it once and it's at an awkward angle. Let's ask Ann.

Ann Says: *'It was a rose, surrounded by some shrubbery. The tattoo is significant because it's the only time we have a hint of Pernille's past. I had decided, with Bjarne, that Pernille had got herself into a spot of bother when she was younger. She was taking drugs and Theis comes along and saves her. The drug dealer Theis kills was the person feeding Pernille's habit.'*

✳ **Fun Fact:** Piv Bernth, the Producer, had no idea that that tattoo wasn't real.

So Theis did **kill that drug dealer?**

Bjarne Says: *'Yes. He did. But they didn't have enough evidence to put him away.'*

So explain the 'incident in the summer' to me please.
Nanna got a secret job at Boils, the nightclub, working with Charlotte (Aunt Lotte), but Theis and Pernille didn't know. When she was there, she was using the Boils dating website, where she met Jens Holck. They had an affair. Her attendance became more erratic and one day Nanna didn't turn up for her shift. Lotte was worried and called Theis. They found Nanna in a hotel room, where she was so drunk she had to be taken to hospital. They never told Pernille.

Ann Says: *'This was a clever subplot because it made me think that the killer might be Theis. In fact I thought it was him for the longest time.'*

Bjarne Says: *'I was really worried it was me. It would have been such a terrible betrayal. I was so relieved when we read the last two episodes. I was off the hook.'*

※ **Fun Fact:** Bjarne's favourite scene from Series 1 is the one in which Pernille can't decide what to wear for Nanna's funeral. *'It makes me want to cry just remembering it'.*

Why didn't Pernille's sister pipe up about Nanna having had a boyfriend at Boils? I mean, she'd only been murdered. Is she really that thick?
Yes. Yes she is.

And for that matter, why didn't Theis say anything?

Bjarne Says: *'Nanna was off the rails during that summer. Theis knew if Pernille knew it would break her. Theis is constantly battling between being the tough guy and a modern man. He had ways of doing things in the past that wouldn't be acceptable now. He's had a tough past. So has Pernille. He was a bad boy.'*

Actually, Theis doesn't really say anything, does he?

Bjarne Says: *'I found this character very quickly. He is a man of few words. He doesn't need to always be talking. When you're in grief, you don't talk so much. You go silent. They wanted me to be more aggressive at the start and I said, no, this is not the way for Theis. He is inward-looking. He doesn't want to show what he's going through.'*

Pernille doesn't like Lund much, does she?

Ann Says: *'No. Neither she nor Theis like the police. I think Pernille would have quite enjoyed slapping Sarah Lund.'*

 **Sofie Says:** 'She should get in line behind everyone else who wants to slap Sarah Lund. A few of my male colleagues moan sometimes that they're not being as clever as Sarah Lund. "I can't believe I'm being this stupid", they say to me. "I can", I reply.'

Is it true that they had to change the killer after the first ten episodes because a cast member accidentally let slip who it was?

No. This is an urban myth. It was a rumour started by a Danish newspaper. It's not true. The writer and producer knew who the killer was from the off. But nobody in the cast knew. They didn't know till the very end. A fax was accidentally sent to the Production Office when they were filming Episode 2 saying the killer was Vagn, but the cast members who knew about this were quickly told it wasn't true.

Nicolaj Says: 'It might have been an accident but if it wasn't then I think it was clever that they did this. Because we still weren't sure, and from that moment on, I had doubt in my mind. And it helped me make choices about what I was doing.'

Sofie Says: 'In the first series, I was really pissed off that they wouldn't tell us who it was, but by the end I embraced it and now I'm glad I didn't know. It doesn't affect my acting at all but it's like reading a crime novel. Each episode is like a new chapter and it keeps your appetite up. You might sooner be bored. But the curiosity of not knowing where the story goes keeps you engaged.'

Whom is Buchard protecting? And who keeps ringing him? And who told him to remove that number from Nanna's phone?

It's the top brass at Police HQ who at this stage are murky figures. They don't want a connection to City Hall.

Morten Says: '*The number was deleted prior to the discovery of the flat so the top brass don't realize that the number is going to be significant. Once it's discovered it is, Buchard has to take the blame. He's the fall guy.*'

※ *Fun Fact:* We'll get to see some of these mysterious bosses in Series 3.

Why has nobody told Knud Padde about his hair?

The wet perm is still acceptable in Danish society. But only just.

Given that what Rahman was actually doing is less bad than raping and murdering one of his own students, why doesn't he pipe up at the first opportunity?

In Denmark it's forbidden to have anything to do with a student out of school, so the fact Nanna turned up at his house was a real problem. Also he has a pregnant wife and he's protecting her. But yes, take your point. The fellah should have piped up pronto.

Given that the blood on the yellow top wouldn't have matched Nanna's, why didn't they wait for results from forensics before jumping to conclusions?

Sometimes it takes 72 hours to get DNA results and Lund and the team had to move fast. They were giddy goats. It's understandable. Also they couldn't wait 72 hours. That's another three episodes, for Pete's sake.

Hang on. Rahman used the same campaign car as the one Nanna was found in? What?

Yes. This is true. As a Role Model, he had access to the City Hall car pool. The Role Models normally get to use the slightly older cars but there were none available so he was given one of the smarter campaign cars instead. But this was a long time ago. He didn't drive the campaign car on the night Nanna was abducted.

The whole car thing. WOW it's so complicated.

Not really. So John Lynge drives the car to the school to deliver leaflets but he comes down with a sudden vomiting bug and thinks he's lost the keys. He hasn't lost the keys. They're still in the car. *Then* a City Hall worker just so happens to be wandering past and notices the car and the keys in it. He drives it off, fills it up with petrol and then takes it back to City Hall. *Then* (try and keep up) Troels, hell-bent on going down in a drunken haze and killing himself, takes the car and drives it to the flat. He then gets plastered and gets a cab, leaving the Party car at the flat, and drives off to the log cabin to stick his head in an oven. Vagn then arrives at the flat, rapes Nanna and uses the car to drive her to Theis's new house and then to the woods, where he puts Nanna in the boot and dumps it in the river.

See? SIMPLE.

Vagn helps Theis kidnap Rahman but when Theis is beating him up and Lund turns up, he's disappeared. Where's he gone?

He tries to get Theis to stop but he won't let up. Vagn runs off because he's scared.

Who took the surveillance tape and when?
It was Morten. He took it Saturday morning after he'd cleaned the flat. The man's an absolute menace.

But if he went to the trouble of stealing it so it wouldn't be found, why does he then send it to Sarah Lund?
At this point in the story everyone thinks the killer is Jens Holck, so the tape is sent because it shows Jens and Nanna together. Morten considers it a final line to be drawn under the case. He thinks his man is in the clear. The dirty rascal.

Who cut the wire outside Lund's flat and who rings her and remains silent?
It was the Policeman With No Name (the one Lund pulls the gun on in Episode 20). He was working for Rie, who was paying him to send info back to City Hall, and she wanted Lund placed under surveillance.

Isn't it THRILLING to know this?

Please explain what happened in Latvia.
Bremer took an all-party trip to Latvia. It was a mixture of businessmen and politicians. Phillip Dessau was with him, as was Jens Holck. Bremer fiddled his expenses when he was out there. Everyone knows about it but nothing was done. More importantly, 21 phone calls were made to Nanna's phone, so whoever made the calls was having the affair with Nanna.

How come nobody from the Party had been in the flat for two weeks?

The toilet was broken.

But wasn't a new toilet meant to be fitted? Who cancelled the toilet?

It wasn't cancelled. Morten just didn't let the workman in.

How come Troels and Rie aren't in massive amounts of trouble for wasting police time? They fabricated an alibi. Isn't that illegal?

It is illegal. There's a never-seen Episode 21 in which Erik Salin, the journalist, blows the whole thing apart and everyone goes to jail. (That last bit might not be true.)

Lars Says: '*I think the reason it isn't pursued is because Troels and Lund are bonded. They are two very lonely people who have put everything they have into their work. I was very disappointed there wasn't a full-blown romance between the pair of them. It felt so good between the two characters. He really wanted to bond with her and she leads him along.*'

Marie Says: '*They are so committed to winning the election they'll do anything. One lie follows another. He's got his secrets and she is very ambitious on his behalf. They've got tunnel vision about it.*'

✳ *Fun Fact:* Marie based the character of Rie on her own sister, '*Not because she is ruthless or anything but because she is so so efficient and is amazing at everything she does.*'

Why does Troels have four pairs of identical shoes?
I'm going to stick my neck out and suggest Troels has OCD.
There. I've said it.

Lars Says: 'He doesn't buy his own clothes or shoes. Rie
bought him two pairs and Morten bought two pairs and
they were the same. It's a work thing. Having said that, I do
the exact same thing. I always buy multiples of things.'

**So Troels is in prison, he's been charged with murder and
all he wants from his lawyer is a copy of the statutes of the
Electoral Commission?** Really?
Yes. Really. He is a stickler for the rules, our Troels (TROO-
OOOEEEEEELS).

Lars Says: 'He's in denial. If it came out that a politician
had tried to commit suicide that would be it. He'd be
finished. He's so secretive, such a closed in character.'

Marie Says: 'I thought the murder was going to come
back to Troels and that Rie was also somehow in on it. It
could have worked, especially with the discovery of the
photograph which shows Troels and Nanna together. They
could have had an affair and Nanna could have threatened
to expose him with the election coming up. Troels would
have killed her for it.'

**Why did Troels call himself Faust on the dating website?
It's hardly a name to inspire romance.**
Faust is a fictional character from a classic German legend.
He's a deeply dissatisfied brainiac who makes a deal with the
devil, giving up his soul in exchange for unlimited knowledge

and pleasure. The word 'Faustian' describes an arrangement whereby a person of ambition surrenders moral integrity in order to achieve power and success. In Goethe's version of the story, Faust, helped by Mephistopheles, seduces a beautiful and innocent maiden who is destroyed by the association. Do I really need to carry on? The whole thing is dripping with metaphorical significance.

The whole stealing of the dating profile thing. I don't get that bit. Please explain it slowly.

OK. So Troels (TROOOOOOELLLLLS) was using the dating website. He left his laptop at the flat and left his profile open. Along comes Jens Holck, finds the laptop, uses it and steals the profile. So Jens Holck was *also* Faust. He was the *bad* Faust. Troels was the good Faust. Think of it like that. It helps.

Why oh why oh why does Holck kill Olav?

Yes. This is puzzling. Olav, who has been exposed, is about to spill the beans on everything that's been going on. But at the *very* worst, all Holck has done is use a flat on the sly to bang a girl he's having an affair with, and has paid a civil servant to facilitate that for him whilst pretending it was for Bremer all along. That's it. He hasn't murdered Nanna. He's been mildly corrupt. So quite why he feels Olav has to die is anyone's guess.

See also: stress.

I love how, after the kidnap scene with Holck, paramedics take Lund's blood pressure through the Jumper.

Yes. I love that too.

: Sofie Says: *'They're actually taking the blood pressure of*
: *the Jumper. Not Lund. They're just checking it's OK.'*

Why doesn't Sarah Lund look at that file of related killings for over a week?

She's been busy! Shut up! Stop moaning.

Why did Brix tell Lund not to connect Nanna's death with Mette Hauge's? Is he mad? Or corrupt?

It's a matter of not losing face for the police case. It was an 18-year-old unsolved case and it's embarrassing. I mean, they're *really* embarrassed about it.

Morten Says: *'He wanted promotion and at the time the department wasn't very effective. He's just doing what he's told. Somebody from upstairs has told him to make this go away.'*

Explain who Gert Stokke is again please and why he's important?

Stokke worked for Holck's department. He found out that Holck was using Troels's flat when he wasn't allowed. He reported this to Bremer. Bremer told him he would have a word with Holck but he did nothing. He also told Stokke not to put any of the discussion in the official meeting minutes. But Stokke did make a note of them and they were tucked away as Appendix 13X.

What this means is that Bremer was aware of Holck's wrongdoing months before any of the murder business came to light. It also, more importantly, means Bremer could have helped Troels out with the police. But he didn't.

I am not entirely clear why Leon runs away given he hasn't done anything wrong. Why does he?

He's scared to death of Vagn and he doesn't want to be questioned by the police. Plus, he has a terribly suspicious face. It's in his DNA to run away. Suspiciously.

What did Vagn want to get from the unit in the warehouse? And how did he know it was there?

He wanted to remove a Year 10 photo from Mette's albums. He's in the back row and it is the only photographic evidence to link him directly to Mette. When Mette was killed he was working for Merkur, the removal firm so chances are it was he who moved the stuff into the unit in the first place.

How did Vagn know to go and get the school photo out of the book in the box and why didn't he do it after the first murder was investigated?

The necklace wasn't an issue after the first murder as there was no body found. He only realizes it's a problem after Lund shows him a picture of Mette. At that point he knows he has to cover up any association with her.

Is it quite funny that Lund arms herself with a candlestick in the warehouse?

I prefer to use the term 'endearing'.

Sofie Says: *'I felt so stupid, when we table-read these episodes. Had it been Bruce Willis it might have worked, but it was a bit ridiculous because it's me. The minute you pick up a candlestick to fight then you put an image of her fighting with a candlestick. I couldn't fight anyone.'*

Why did Jan Meyer not identify Vagn? He had met him and knew who he was. Wouldn't it have been better for him to say 'It was Vagn' rather than mutter an obscure clue, 'Sara 84', on a loop?

He's just been shot twice, had life-saving surgery and is off his tits on morphine. Cut the man some slack.

The shooter is right-handed. But Vagn is left-handed. (He writes the birthday card for the Teletubbies with his left hand.) Explain that.

He is ambidextrous. Basic.

Why has that Police Prosecutor got such a bug up his arse?

He's just had a vasectomy and his testicles are terribly sore and he's worried he may never have sex again. Oh hang on. That's not *The Killing*. That's *The Bridge*.

Well spotted.

Thanks.

Why did Leon kill himself?

He didn't. Vagn killed him. He had a blow to the head before he was hanged. Do keep up.

Why does Anton find his dead sister's passport and think 'Oh I know, I'll put it back where I found it. I don't need to tell my parents about this.'

He needs a clip round the ear. Plus he's livid with his parents for not using his name.

How did Nanna's passport end up in the cupboard? And why didn't Vagn get rid of it?

It's safe to assume that Vagn didn't know it was there. He went to great lengths to clean the basement so wouldn't have left something so incriminating. The passport fell out during one of their struggles and slipped under the cupboard door.

Did Rie cheat on Troels?

Wellllll. She tells Troels she didn't. She says she went out for a drink with Phillip Dessau and they wound up in his hotel room but they didn't have sexy horseplay. That's what she tells Troels. But . . .

Marie Says: *'She did cheat on him. She cheated on him bad. And then, after he chucked her, she did it with Phillip Dessau again. She's a girl who will do anything to get what she wants.'*

Why doesn't Rie stick up for herself and why doesn't Troels reinstate her after he knows the truth?

Morten makes Troels believe she was the one leaking the info. His trust in her has gone and she accepts it. Power has destroyed him. He's no longer the man she was in love with. Having said that, just having her say *'Troels! Troels!'* doesn't really cut it.

Marie Says: *'I think the writers were probably exhausted by this point. They just wanted her out of the room.'*

The necklace: How come Vagn had it when he killed Nanna? Is it the same necklace he gave Mette, or another one he's bought since?

It's the same necklace. Vagn was wearing the necklace and she ripped it off him in their final fight so he doesn't realize it's clenched in her fist. Otherwise he would have taken it from her.

Nicolaj Says: '*He doesn't know how to handle love. If he loves someone and they don't love him back then he can't control his emotions. He gets angry and this is a guy who hasn't got a stop button. He sees red and he can't stop. The moment he rapes Nanna she has to die. He thinks he owns Nanna. He's watched her grow up. And now, when she's a woman, he's confused. He doesn't know what to do with his feelings. He loves this family but at the same time he resents not having a love of his own. Jealousy runs through him.*'

Sofie Says: '*I realized, during filming, that someone had given me a black heart necklace for my 30th birthday. I'd forgotten about it so when I saw the black necklace they used I was freaked out.*'

Why doesn't Amir recognize Vagn in the line-up? Given he's known the family for years?

He doesn't know Vagn. In fact he doesn't really know the family other than Nanna. They went to school together but that was it.

What's going on with Vagn's hair in the last episode?

This is a mystery as deep as the seas. Except it isn't. In the last episode he's simply not wearing his hat. And he's scrubbed up for the party. That's the answer. Move on.

Nicolaj Says: '*This scene, the Last Supper, was so difficult for me. Here were these boys whom I had loved so much* and I had murdered their sister. I had betrayed Theis and Pernille and I knew what I was going to do. We all found it deeply upsetting.'

Ann Says: 'During this scene, I could feel Pernille's anger and fear in every bone. It was a very hard scene to do. But of course, in a way, she's always known it was Vagn. As for me, I guessed it was Vagn when he arrived at the house bringing pizzas. There was something about it that made me think, "Ahh! It's him."'

Is Anton's birthday party and Uncle Vagn's 'surprise' the worst in living memory?

Yes. Yes it is.

Was it right that Theis kills Vagn?

Well. It depends who you talk to . . .

Bjarne Says: 'For me, it was right. It was an awful, awful ending but it was real. And it was absolutely right for my character that he says nothing to Vagn. He gives him nothing.'

Ann Says: 'I found it very difficult to stand still during that scene in the woods. Every bone in my body wanted to run to Theis and stop him. Actually, I think it would have been better if Pernille had taken the gun from Theis and shot Vagn herself. That would have been very powerful.'

Yes. Pernille killing him would have been awesome.

Sofie Says: 'It took me some time to realize that this was

*the perfect ending. It makes everyone losers. In that sense
it's true to the darkness of the story. It ends where it should.
There are no heroes. No victory for anyone. At first I was
disappointed it was Vagn but then I understood that it
absolutely was the right ending for the story.'*

Fun Fact: When they read the final two episodes,
Bjarne and Nicolaj were working together on a play. On
discovering that he really was the killer, Nicolaj went to
Bjarne, terrified, and told him he was going to have to leave
Denmark.

Nicolaj Says: 'I was so so worried. I thought I was going
to be spat on in the street. But it was OK. People were very
nice.'

Isn't the ending a massive compromise for Troels?

Lars Says: 'He is so conflicted but this is politics and
politics corrupts everyone in the end. Actually, I was
expecting the murder to all come back to me. After I was
charged in Episode 10 we had a filming break for six months
and I thought, oh it can't be me after all, it's too soon. But
then, around Episode 18, I started to think it was going to be
Troels. Actually I would have preferred it to be Troels.'

**Also, he's been charged with murder, he's given an opponent
a heart attack, he's fabricated an alibi and wasted police
time and he's still elected Mayor?**
The Danish are a nonchalant lot. True life.

Lars Says: 'No scandal can touch him. What can I say?

The Danish people are very forgiving . . . and politics is a game.'

✹ **Fun Fact:** Troels is a member of the Radical Left Party, a right-wing political group. Mayor Bremer is a Social Democrat and is left-wing. We're never told that in the show.

What are the three things Brix tells Lund are going to be omitted from the case files?

The allegation that someone was watching her, the allegation that someone was protecting City Hall and the fact that other cases were linked to this one.

I declare shenanigans.

⋮ **Sofie Says:** *'I liked the openness of Lund's ending. That there's no shelf to put her on. It's true to her character. We shouldn't know where she's going.'*

✹ **Fun Fact:** At the end of this scene, Lund had a line as she was standing in the doorway. She said, 'I'll call you'. But this line was cut in the final edit.

So that's Series 1 done and dusted. Let's move on to Series 2 (*rubs thighs*).

✳ ⚬ ✳ ⚬ ✳ **3** ✳ ⚬ ✳ ⚬ ✳

SERIES TWO

It's two years since the end of the Birk Larsen case and Sarah Lund has been demoted. She's working as a Passport Controller in Gedser. A lawyer, Anne Dragsholm, has been found brutally murdered in strange circumstances and Lund's old boss, Lennart Brix, sends for her, asking if she can help solve the case. Sarah pulls on her new jumper (it's red) and heads back to Copenhagen.

In parliament, Thomas Buch has just been appointed the new Minister of Justice. He's been charged with the difficult job of getting the government's new Terrorism Package passed. But details of the Dragsholm case turn up in his briefing documents and Buch finds himself at the centre of a political mystery that goes to the heart of the investigation.

Let's meet the key players . . .

THE POLICE STATION

✳ Ulrik Strange (Mikael Birkkjaer)

I suppose the clue was in the name. What with Meyer gone (oh Meyer, how we loved thee), Lund needs another partner and, given she's been hauled up from Boring Town where she's been grindin' out the days on Dull Detail, she'll take whoever she's given. A silver-tongued fox in the making, Strange has us on the hop from the off. Not taking no for an answer, this Lund Whisperer begins his tentative prowl around our mildly depressed heroine and, against all the odds, manages to stroke her face, peck her on the cheek and then shoot her four times in the chest. If this is how Danish men conduct their courtships then I suggest you stick to Swedes.

He loves: Football and opera
He hates: Hot days and eagle-eyed lawyers
Most likely to say: 'Can I come in for some cake? I mean sex. Obviously.'

Mikael Says: 'He's a psychopath. He wants his Sofie trophy.'

Sofie Says: 'Mikael is the only man I know who does crosswords and smokes a pipe.'

✳ *Fun Fact:* During Episode 4, as Strange and Lund were running through the woods in Skogo, they kept falling over and were unable to stop laughing.

Forbrydelsen *Bingo Points*: He's in *Borgen*

✳ Ruth Hedeby (Lotte Andersen)

Deputy Commissioner, she's at the top end of the middle ring of top brass, the mouthpiece for shadowy forces whom we never see or smell. Not only that, but she's having an affair with Brix. The minx. She spends most of her time telling Brix to take Lund off the case, then put her back on the case, then take her off the case, then put her back on the case, then take her off the case (repeat to fade). She also has the finest collection of casual lady-scarves in Denmark.

She loves: Being the boss of Brix
She hates: Unauthorized trips to Helmand
Most likely to say: 'Meet me at Hotel Rumpypump in an hour.'

Morten Says: 'There's a reason she's so tough on Lund. She's jealous.'

⋮ **Sofie Says:** 'A lot of women in high positions are Alpha
⋮ Females. They feel threatened by other strong women.

Hedeby is an Alpha Female. Lund's not an Alpha. She's a lone wolf so she's not threatened by other women.'

✳ Erik Konig (Søren Pilmark)

Head of Special Branch. Another murky presence in the dark corners of Police HQ. It's a general truth that when someone who is supposed to be in charge is slamming brakes on left, right and centre and refusing to pursue lines of inquiry that are obvious even to a toddler, then they're being leaned on by forces unknown. It's the first rule of police physics.

He loves: Throwing his weight around
He hates: Being proved so wrong it hurts
Most likely to say: 'I was only following orders.'

PARLIAMENT

✳ Thomas Buch (Nicolas Bro)

Newly appointed Minister of Justice, Thomas Buch is only one leaked memo away from triumph or disaster. A fashion trendsetter, he has made the 'jumper under the jacket' a must-have look for gentlemen of a certain size. Slightly highly strung, he deals with stress by bouncing a rubber ball against parliamentary walls, eating sweets from his pockets, biscuits in the back of his car, carrots in his office, takeaways in meeting rooms, more sweets at his desk, sandwiches on the move and, in an emergency, one small pear. If he's not eating, he's cleaning his teeth standing in rooms with no sinks, having conversations with colleagues on his knees in toilets, or calling hastily thought-through press conferences which he then promptly walks out of. He has the aura of a large confused dog.

He loves: Thorough investigations
He hates: Cover-ups and being off his tits on sugar
Most likely to say: 'Are you going to finish that? I'm a bit peckish.'

Nicolas Says: 'When Buch is inevitably voted out of office, he's going to be a teacher. I think he'd be good at that.'

Sofie Says: 'I suggested him for the part so I was really disappointed that I only had one scene with him.'

※ *Fun Fact 1:* Sofie and Nicolas are related. They're third cousins. They've also had a kissing scene. They were in *Macbeth* together. She was Lady Macbeth and he was Macbeth. 'It was weird kissing my cousin.'

※ *Fun Fact 2:* Nicolas was constantly entertained during filming by Charlotte and Preben (who play Karina and Plough) as they are both stars of musical theatre in Denmark and were forever singing show tunes between takes.

※ Karina Munk Jørgensen (Charlotte Guldberg)
Private secretary with the emphasis on 'private'. She's been working in the Ministry of Justice for years and nobody is even vaguely aware that she has one sticky-looking child. You might feel an

instant urge to dismiss her entirely as 'the blonde one in the office' but don't be so hasty – she's got a top drawer of tasty secrets waiting to be gouged out with a truth stick. Karina also does an excellent job of winding Thomas Buch up and then standing back and watching him spin. Her main function seems to be suddenly uncovering crucial memos and accompanying Thomas to the hospital, where she can stand in the background making a sad face.

She loves: Mysterious files
She hates: Having to confess all
Most likely to say: 'Oh, look what I found in the back of this drawer!'

❈ Carsten Plough (Preben Kristensen)

Like all good Permanent Secretaries, Plough sports a pair of exceedingly tidy glasses. Nothing unusual about that, you might think, but in the world of *The Killing*, smart specs tell us one immutable fact – he's clearly up to something. A stickler for parliamentary rules, Plough is never not arranging face time for his Minister with 'the Opposition' or the 'People's Party'. Like a dressage pony who could turn bad in the blink of an eye, Plough can always be relied on to stand in the corner of any conference room and bore holes into political shenanigans with nothing but his staring eyes. In the ever-faithful tradition of Danish political helpers, Plough is merely biding his time until he can reveal his own true, potentially dastardly, intentions.

He loves: Procedure and all it stands for

He hates: Skopje
Most likely to say: 'You're never allowed to go to the Ministry of Integration ever again.'

❋ Frode Monberg (Niels Anders Thorn)

Oh Frode, Frode, Frode. The former Minister of Justice who, after realizing his part in the Big Bad Deed contributed to the death of the woman he's been secretly in love with for over twenty years, has a complete mental breakdown, tries to top himself, fails and ends up in hospital where he has to pretend he's had a bit of a heart attack. He's fooling nobody. Not only that, but he's the whipping boy for Bully Rossing. 'You don't know what he's like,' he whimpers, while standing in a hospital gown with his arse hanging out the back. Is this any way to conduct parliamentary business? No. It isn't.

He loves: Anne Dragsholm
He hates: Tricky questions in his fragile state
Most likely to say: 'Is there any chance you could bring me in some sandwiches? The hospital food is awful.'

❋ Flemming Rossing (Ole Lemmeke)

Evil Minister of Defence. You can tell he's evil because his hair is slicked back and he has a nonchalant, almost haughty approach to jackets. In fact he is *so* evil, you wouldn't bat an eyelid if he quietly unfurled plans for the Death Star. He's the Flashman of the Danish government, bullying ministers and riding roughshod over the truth – but mostly, he's got the biggest nose in Denmark. It's a proper hooter. Respect.

He loves: Narrowing his eyes suspiciously
He hates: Severed hands
Most likely to say: 'If you don't do what I say, I'll give you a Chinese burn. Again.'

The Prime Minister (Kurt Ravn)

He's so important he doesn't even need a name. On the face of it, he's like an affable uncle. He likes to eat sandwiches standing in his shirtsleeves and he's got two soft, watery blue eyes that say 'Hello. Now trust me.' Don't be fooled. Nobody got to be Prime Minister by being a boy scout and, like most men of power, this fellah is pulling all the strings. In the fair and true tradition of the dastardly politician, he's ticking all the boxes – appointing someone he specifically wants to be useless, keeping the slimy one close at all times and juggling with the truth like a street con artist. Don't go near him with a bargepole.

He loves: Being top dog
He hates: Implausible deniability
Most likely to say: 'These are not the files you're looking for.'

Nicolaj Says: *'He's based on a real Danish Prime Minister who was as hard as ice.'*

✳ Erling Krabbe (Jens Jacob Tychsen)

Leader of the People's Party. The thorn in Buch's side, he's hell bent on scuppering the mysterious Terrorism Package and bringing the Minister of Justice to his knees during which, ironically, a scene in a toilet, he manages to achieve. He has also, to Buch's immense surprise, got a really hot wife.

He loves: Cracking down on terrorism
He hates: Ahl Al Kahf
Most likely to say: 'Do you mind? I'm trying to have a poo.'

✳ Birgitte Agger (Benedikte Hansen)

Leader of the Opposition. We don't know much about Birgitte Agger, except she's the Opposition. That's it. She just wanders about being Opposite to everything. Like a finger and a hole, she's in, out, in, out, in for a bit more, then out again when it comes to that pesky Terrorism Package. She should make her mind up! Yeah. That's told her.

She loves: Pacing across a room
She hates: Not being in the loop secret-wise
Most likely to say: 'I don't know what it is, but I am opposite to it.'
Forbrydelsen Bingo Points: She's in *Borgen*

THE BARRACKS
....

✳ Colonel Torsten Jarnvig (Flemming Enevold)
Battalion Commander of Team Aegir, Head of Barracks, dad to

Louise, looks like he might make intricate to-scale replica model villages in his spare time. No nonsense and to the point, he's your archetypal Dad in charge of loads of men in uniform. Probably smells of pies and pipes. Like all good men of honour, he's not averse to bending the rules to do the right thing. Love him for this.

He loves: A ship-shape manoeuvre
He hates: Deleted radio signals
Most likely to say: 'I'm turning a blind eye now, while you escape through a door that I may or may not be coincidentally gesturing towards with my nose.'

※ **Fun Fact:** Flemming is a massive musical theatre star in Denmark and played the Phantom to great critical acclaim.

※ Major Christian Søgaard (Carsten Bjørnlund)

The blond bombshell of Team Aegir. Second in command at Ryvangen Army Barracks, Søgaard likes nothing better than to answer penetrating questions while standing in a shower butt naked with his hands on his hips. It's the Danish way. He's the man with his eye on the prize – namely, banging the boss's daughter, which he manages with admirable enthusiasm. He also sports a tidy moustache for which he should be applauded. He can kill a man with one finger.

He loves: Louise Raben

He hates: Jens Raben
Most likely to say: 'Pass me the soap. And that list of questions.'
Forbrydelsen *Bingo Points*: He's in *Those Who Kill*

✲ Said Bilal (Igor Radosavljevic)

Watch out everyone! It's a soldier who is also a Muslim! Sound the klaxon of suspicion! He's got to be up to no good? Right? Well shame on you. Because Bilal is as upstanding a fellow as you would ever hope to meet in a barracks besieged by multiple deaths and dark secrets. The fact that he aids and abets a murky cover-up, kidnaps his boss's daughter and then blows himself up suicide bomber-style is neither here nor there. He was a good'un. Just misunderstood. And a bit unstable.

He loves: The army
He hates: Anyone who doesn't love the army or says bad things about the army
Most likely to say: 'Just leave the army alone! And to prove my point, I will now explode this massive device.'

✲ Louise Raben (Stine Praetorius)

Poster girl of the Ryvangen Barracks, married to Jens, daughter of Colonel Jarnvig, mother of small, permanently frowning boy and, for one night only, banger of Christian Søgaard. The air of sorrow hangs over her like a cloud, not helped by the fact that she stares at people in a confused manner as if everyone is forever trying to explain quantum physics to her. Never knowingly blinks. Must stand at least two metres from Sarah Lund at all times.

She loves: Packing things into boxes
She hates: Visiting that bloody hospital
Most likely to say: 'So hang on. Explain that again. Is he mental or not mental? I'm having trouble keeping up.'

✲ General Arild (Finn Nielsen)

All dark forces need a shadowy leader and in General Arild, the Danish army has a perfect murky manager. His aim: to protect the army's reputation at all costs. Never mind the overwhelming evidence that a former Special Forces soldier has gone crackalackdingdong and is bumping people off willy-nilly. Far more important that a gruesome incident be hidden behind a curtain of discretion and innocent ex-servicemen are allowed to be brutally murdered than let anyone think one single bad thought about the Danish Army. Ever. Always beware the man in charge who comes smiling.

He loves: Things swept under carpets
He hates: Having to explain civilian fatalities
Most likely to say: 'It was only *one* family. *One*. There's no need to bang on about it.'

THOSE OTHER CHARACTERS

··

✳ Anne Dragsholm (Sarah Gottlieb)

Victim number one. The lawyer for 3-2-Alpha Squadron. Back in the day, Dragsholm was the woman tasked with representing soldiers charged with war crimes. She got them off but never stopped believing there *had* been an atrocity committed and that someone needed to jolly well do something about it. With a legal bee in her bonnet, Dragsholm asks for the case to be reopened but hoowee, look at the trouble it causes. All she wanted was to do her job properly. That was it. And what does she get for it? Beaten up, strapped to a chair and stabbed 21 times. It's the worst performance-related bonus *ever*.

She loves: Wielding the sword of justice
She hates: Being filmed with no make-up on
Most likely to say: 'Excuse me, are you the officer everyone keeps telling me killed all those civilians?'

✳ Jens Raben (Ken Vedsegaard)

The most forgetful man in the Danish Army. Squadron leader of 3-2-Alpha. Once a promising young officer, his life has been decimated by an incident that may or may not have happened. Suffering from Post Traumatic Stress Disorder, Raben has been institutionalized for two long years and, to be honest, he's had enough. Pushed to breaking point by the dreadful mural of a wood he's forced to stare at every time someone comes to visit, Raben takes matters into his own hands and escapes using the old *Shawshank Redemption* method of crawling out through a sewer. He then spends the rest of his time trying slowly but surely to remember stuff as all his mates are bumped off one by one in alarming circumstances.

He loves: Louise, Jonas and the sweet smell of freedom
He hates: Taking his pills
Most likely to say: 'How many times do I have to tell you? It's *him.*'

❊ Allan Myg Poulsen (Nicolai Dahl Hamilton)

Victim number two. Member of 3-2-Alpha. Chapter secretary for the ex-servicemen's club. You know what it's like. You're involved in a wartime atrocity, everything goes to hell, you start to get your life back and then boom. You're hunted down by a psycopath, hung up by your feet and killed like a pig. Such. Bad. Luck.

He loves: That mural. He thinks it's really neat.
He hates: Bumping into *that* officer
Most likely to say: 'Oh OK. If you want to join the ex-servicemen's club then we can go to my warehouse and you can fill in a form and I can . . . ow!'

❊ David Grüner (Johan Philip Asbaek)

Victim number three. Member of 3-2-Alpha. Wounded in combat, Grüner is now in a wheelchair. He's managed to get himself sorted with a nice little night-time security job. Too bad he's going to die in circumstances *so* appalling Sarah Lund has to puke up in a bucket slung over the back of a tap. It's what they like to call 'a very bad business'.

He loves: The quiet life
He hates: Staring at a mobile phone whilst doused in petrol

Mostly likely to say: 'Why did I disable the sprinklers? *Why?*'
Forbrydelsen *Bingo Points:* He's in *Borgen*

✳ Priest (Lars Sidenius)

Victim number four. Priest in charge at St Simon's Church, Vesterbro. Army chaplain given to wearing fancy ruffs, he's the Priest With No Name. The keeper of secrets, this holy man not only fibs about Anne Dragsholm, but he's not averse to pulling a gun for no reason either. He's the go-to man for all the members of 3-2-Alpha trying to get in touch with each other. Shifty and slightly slippery, Priest pays the price for his tight-lipped approach to a string of murders. Foolish.

He loves: The baby Jesus
He hates: The smell of trouble
Most likely to say: 'No. I'm not a Scientologist.'

✳ Frederik Holst (Mads Wille)

Brother of Sebastian Holst, member of 3-2-Alpha killed during the incident. Surgeon based in Helmand, he's positively livid with the surviving members of his brother's squadron. The sender of the medical report that started this whole sorry mess, Frederik wanted the squadron to be convicted of war crimes. They weren't. So he just angrily put crosses through their faces every time he heard one of them was dead. Like you do.

He loves: His dead brother
He hates: 3-2-Alpha Squadron
Most likely to say: 'Random severed hand! Hello! Anyone?'

✳ ***Fun Fact:*** His real name is Mads Wille. MADS WILLE. (I am 45 years old.)

❋ Connie Vemmer (Hanne Hedelund)

Chain-smoking journalist who uncovers the whiff of decay and wants something done about it. Has a flagrant disregard for No Smoking signs; she's also much given to running purposefully up and down stairs after ministers shaking files in their faces. While smoking.

She loves: Smoking
She hates: Not smoking
Most likely to say: 'Have you got a light?'

❋ Per K Moller

Blown up by a massive bomb, poor Per is the most wronged man in Danish military history. He has his identity stolen, is blamed for a dreadful wartime atrocity and then, just to rub salt in the wound, is dug up and picked over. Sarah Lund actually tries to pull one of the teeth from his skull at one point. Poor old Per. He's so dead.

He loves: Eternal peace
He hates: Being dug up like an old bone
Most likely to say: 'Wooooooooooooooooooooh'

Sofie Says: 'We dug up dead actors for this role. We take casting very seriously.'

❋ Lisbeth Thomsen (Lotte Munk Fure)

Victim number six. Member of 3-2-Alpha. A shunner of the city lights, Lisbeth has moved to the Swedish island of Skogo where she's holed herself up in a log cabin and intends to keep herself to herself till further notice. Except she can't because she's on the wanted list of a ruthless killer. Which is a shame, because apparently she's amazing at chopping logs.

She loves: The smell of pine in the mornings
She hates: Bombs in her cupboards
Most likely to say: 'No. I don't know who rigged up that odd-looking hide either.'

✲ Kodmani (Ramadan Husseini)

Shadowy mastermind behind Ahl Al Kahf, a Muslim political group. Contacted by the mysterious Faith Fellow, Kodmani is clearly quite trusting as he sets up a PO box for him, no questions asked. Spends much of his time in a hidden basement on the internet, like most overweight men with beards.

He loves: Allah
He hates: The decadent West
Most likely to say: 'Allah ha akbar!'

Those Pesky Plot Holes

At the end of the first episode someone is running away from the warehouse where they find Myg's body. But Strange is with Lund. Who is it?

It's Bilal. He went to the warehouse to confront Myg because someone had hacked the barracks database. They thought it might be him.

But why did he run away? He didn't kill him so what was he afraid of? And why didn't he call the police when he found the body? Like a normal person?

He had some of Myg's blood on his trousers and was clearly worried about being found at the scene of a murder by police officers. But you're right. He panicked.

When Strange goes to the barracks, how come not one single person recognizes him, given he was a soldier in Afghanistan at the same time as all of Team Aegir?

He only met 3-2-Alpha Squadron. He wasn't hanging with the boys. He just likes hanging the boys.

Mikael Says: 'He wasn't part of Team Aegir. He was part of a top secret Special Forces operation. Nobody was supposed to know he was there. The only people who would have been able to identify him were the members of 3-2-Alpha Squadron who were involved in the incident with the civilians.'

So how come Lisbeth Thomsen doesn't recognize him? She was part of 3-2-Alpha Squadron?

Because she was sent back to barracks with the wounded. She didn't go with the others to the village. So she never saw Strange.

OK. So who was Team Aegir?

Team Aegir was a battalion of 500 soldiers sent to Afghanistan.

And 3-2-Alpha Squadron were a part of Team Aegir?

Correct.

And who was in 3-2-Alpha?

Eight people were in the squad. Jens Raben – he was squadron leader – Myg, Grüner, Lisbeth Thomsen, HC, Sebastian Holst, Bo, and one unnamed soldier who was killed in the armoured vehicle attack.

Who's Bo?

He was in the armoured vehicle they were in when they crossed the bridge on their way to the village. They'd received a distress call from another unit nearby but the vehicle was attacked on the bridge. Bo was injured. Lisbeth stayed with the wounded to be picked up by helicopter. The others went on to the village. Bo dies. It's a bad business.

Was there a radio distress call and was there another squad under attack or not?

Yes. There was a distress call. But it wasn't another squad. It was Strange, on his own. But he was wearing Per K Moller's dogtags and calling himself Perk. The sneaky puss.

So who deleted the radio call and why?

It was Bilal acting under orders from General Arild. They didn't want it getting out that Danish soldiers had murdered civilians. It was a cover-up.

Can you explain precisely what happened in the village?

Yes. Five days before the incident, 3-2-Alpha get a message from a Special Forces squad asking for assistance. Raben has been to the village many times and, according to Sebastian Holst's video diary, has become obsessed with a particular family whom he believes to be Taliban informers. The squad don't want to go but are forced to by Raben. On the way, their armoured vehicle is blown up. Bo gets a gun barrel up into his throat and two others are wounded. A helicopter is called to pick up the wounded. Lisbeth Thomsen stays with them. Raben then leads Myg, Grüner, Sebastian and HC to the village where they find a single Special Forces officer calling himself Perk who is holed up in a house with the family Raben claims may be Taliban informers. They remain under attack and can't escape. They run low on water. Strange wants to get hold of a radio and tells the father of the family to fetch him one. But he is unable to do so. Then, according to whom you believe, either Raben or Strange takes the youngest daughter and shoots her in the head. (It was Raben.) Then Strange kills the mother, then the son and then the father. The bodies are placed inside the large bread oven that's in the house. And that's it.

What happened in the two years between Strange leaving the army and joining the police force?

It was a slow process of changing from the military to the police. He was in the elite Special Forces. He wanted to be a police officer and General Arild made that happen.

Why does Søgaard deny knowing Anne Dragsholm? Wasn't she a member of Team Aegir?

No. She wasn't. But she did go to the barracks to give a few lectures to the soldiers and she did represent 3-2-Alpha Squadron in their disciplinary hearing. He wouldn't have remembered her.

Why does Sarah Lund's mother have a lamp on in a room with two massive windows in the middle of the day?

Finally! This explains why everywhere else in Denmark

is so dark and nobody has their lights on. She's draining the grid.

Sofie Says: *'Actually, it's very common to have the lights on in the day. It's very Scandinavian. We're so desperate for daylight. To be honest, I think Sarah just forgot to turn it off. She also leaves the seat up on the toilet . . . That last bit might be a joke.'*

Why does Brix give the order not to pursue the Faith Fellow lead?

It's a bad call. But he thinks Lund and Strange need to concentrate on the members of Team Aegir. At this point, they don't think Faith Fellow is a soldier.

Morten Says: *'He's working on hunches all the time. If he feels a line of inquiry is a dead end then he tells them to stop. But it's also a balancing act with Lund. He knows if he says no, it makes her work faster. Sometimes he stops her to motivate her. And she almost always ignores everything Brix tells her anyway. It's reverse psychology. She's got a one-track mind and he wants her not to waste time.'*

But Faith Fellow is the source of the video of Anne Dragsholm! He's clearly the killer! Is Brix mad?

Brix moves in mysterious ways. Plus, if Brix wasn't so wrong, Sarah Lund wouldn't be so right. Suck it up.

Morten Says: *'Deep down Brix knows full well Lund is a much better detective than he will ever be. Whenever every trace and track seem to come to an end, she knows there's* *always something that's been overlooked. To be honest, Brix is a terrible detective. He's a middle manager.'*

So if Strange was Faith Fellow, what was he trying to do?

It's your classic diversionary tactic. He gets a radical Muslim group to set up a PO box into which he then places incriminating evidence. Namely the dogtags and the list of Team Aegir members.

So he's trying to frame them?

Precisely. He's trying to make it look like terrorism.

Doesn't he do that again? With Søgaard?

Yes. He does. When he realizes the framing of Kodmani and Ahl Al Kahf hasn't worked, he needs to pin it on someone else. So he places the dogtags in Søgaard's locker. He's a one-trick pony, to be honest.

He's playing a dangerous game though, isn't he? Isn't he the one who tells Brix that Lund should investigate Raben even though Brix doesn't want her to?

Yes. But at this point, he's trying to stitch up Raben as well. Also, he's trying to find all the members of 3-2-Alpha himself. So he can kill them. He just wants to kill them.

Mikael Says: '*Also, at this point I had absolutely no idea I was the killer. Although I did start getting suspicious because Strange kept getting sent out of scenes.'*

Blimey. He's rotten to the core isn't he?

Yes. He's a proper wrong'un. He is ice-cold and manipulative. And really, really handsome. Which is annoying.

Is it true Brix is secretly in love with Lund?

Morten Says: '*He's having an affair with Ruth Hedeby. It'd be a very tricky threesome. Brix is Lund's champion and he is fascinated with her but he's not in love with her. He's too scared to be in love with her. Ruth Hedeby would have his balls for toast.'*

Why does Jens Raben deny knowing Anne Dragsholm? Everyone's denying knowing her. What's that about?
He doesn't want to get involved, he just wants to escape and lead a normal life.

Who leaked the memo to Birgitte Agger?
It was Plough. He was determined to get to the bottom of what happened to his son in Afghanistan.

Hang on. Remind me again. Which one was Plough's son?
We never see him. He was the one called HC. He went to the village with 3-2-Alpha and was present during the killing of the civilians. He came back, became depressed and killed himself by driving the wrong way up a motorway. And Plough wanted the investigation reopened.

Where did Raben get his wire-cutters from? How come he's allowed to walk unaccompanied between wards?
Raben secreted the tool from the workshop where he worked. As for the lack of security, the hospital has a pretty relaxed vibe. They might want to tighten that up.

Can you explain precisely what the Terrorism Package is proposing to do?

No. No I can't.

Nicolas Says: 'In Denmark it's a fundamental right to be able to have free meetings. The People's Party are angling to have that right restricted so that certain Muslim groups are no longer able to gather freely. Buch is fighting this.'

✳ *Fun Fact:* To prepare for the role, Nicolas spent two days at the Ministry of Justice following the Minister around. The first time he went he was following a woman who had been in the job for seven years and was extremely efficient. The second time he visited he was following the new Minister for Justice, who happened to be on his first day of the job, just like Buch.

And why would a memo from Special Branch briefing a minister that the killings may be linked to terrorism make the Opposition pull out of their support for the Terrorism Package? Surely that would make them want a Terrorism Package more?

Well, yes. You would be right to think that. But they are the Opposition. This is what they do.

Nicolas Says: 'Also, Agger's party are against the war in Iraq from the start. It's parliamentary politics. They're saying, "This is your war, not ours. We're having nothing to do with it."'

Why did Monberg remove the memo from the file anyway?
It contained sensitive information that might jeopardize national security, but mostly because Bully Rossing told him to.

What sensitive information?
You know . . . about the severed hand that didn't belong to any Danish soldier and was proof that civilians had been killed. Basically, they didn't want it getting out that Danish soldiers had committed war crimes.

Why not?
Two reasons. First, the Prime Minister wanted to be head of the UN but he needed the backing of the Americans to do it. And in order to get the support of the Americans, the Prime Minister needed to pass legislation in parliament increasing spending on the military so he could send more troops to Afghanistan. If news of Danish soldiers committing war crimes had got out before that vote, he would have failed.

So the Danish Prime Minister is a right piece of work? Is that what you're saying?
Yes. Yes I am.

I'm a bit confused about the whole trail of paper at the Ministry, to be honest. Can you explain it?
It all starts with a medical report faxed to the Ministry of Defence in August. The fax has been sent by Frederik Holst. A severed hand was found amongst the remains of the dead Danish soldiers. It's covered in henna, as is the custom amongst the Hazara tribe (who hate the Taliban) and has a gold ring on one finger. (The Taliban do not wear gold.)

Therefore, this severed hand belongs to a civilian, backing up claims that a war crime has been committed by Danish forces.

Nothing is done for two months.

A second medical report is faxed in October in which it is claimed the hand belongs to a suicide bomber. And so the cover-up begins . . .

Monberg posts the file on the incident to the Ministry. He does that because he wants to clear his conscience and then he tries to kill himself.

Plough puts the Dragsholm file into Buch's notes. He also leaks Monberg's Special Branch memo. He also makes sure Karina finds Monberg's second diary.

Nicolas Says: 'It's typical to have two diaries. One is for public duties, the other for private appointments. It's the private one that Plough puts in Karina's way.'

Why doesn't Grüner tell Raben about Perk or the incident when they meet in the church? Two people have died.

They're all trying to forget and move on. Grüner has a wife and child and he wants to get back to leading a normal life. Having said that, it's pretty obvious that members of 3-2-Alpha are being bumped off, you'd think the remaining ones would all get together, stand in a circle and scream 'Who is doing this? *We really need to work it out.'*

These murders are shaping up to be pretty gruesome aren't they?

Utterly revolting, yes.

Mikael Says: 'They're brutal – he's sick. He's a charming psychopath. As the series went on, there were bets on who the killer was in Copenhagen and suddenly, towards the end, the betting went up massively on it being me. Men in bars were constantly shouting "It's YOU!" at me.'

Sofie Says: *'It's a brutal story. At first I felt it was wrong. At times it felt we were telling a story faster, quicker to be sensational, but it would have been the easiest thing to simply copy Series 1. So Series 2 is moving on. We didn't want to do the same thing. Søren took the universe of* The Killing, *was true to its darkness but did something different.'*

Why did the husband confess to Anne Dragsholm's murder?
He's out of his mind with grief. And according to him, he is past caring what the police think of him. All that matters to him is that Anne knows he didn't kill her.

But of course Anne knows he didn't kill her. Because he didn't.
Don't confuse the matter with facts. He's clearly gone a bit mad. His former wife has been stabbed 21 times, for crying out loud. Cut the man some slack.

Was Anne Dragsholm fired from her job? Or did she resign?
She resigned. She wanted the case reopened. And it wasn't happening. So she went off on her own determined to find the rogue soldier who called himself Perk.

OK. So on that, explain the Perk thing again?
Per K Moller was killed in an explosion. Strange took his dogtags and then pretended to be him. He got his dogtags because he was being treated at the same field hospital when Per's body was brought in. He stole them.

What is the document Karina hands out at the consultation explaining the sensitive nature of the leaked memo?
Absolutely no idea. But I do know that its main purpose is to be thrust urgently about the room.

Nicolas Says: 'They constantly have to check that what they're doing is legal. If any minister breaks the law then that's that, they have to go before a judge there and then. The document she produces basically proves to the other parties that the non-disclosure of the memo is perfectly legal and that revealing it would jeopardize the lives of Danish soldiers.'

Who are Ahl Al Kahf and what have they got to do with anything?
They're a Muslim political group the People's Party want banned. Kodmani seems to be a figurehead for them. Their involvement in the case, however, is nil. They've done nothing. They're being stitched up like kippers.

How does Raben know where Grüner works?
Priest told him.

What's the significance of the tyre around Grüner again?
A tyre around a victim is commonly used on informers in South Africa and, more significantly, American security personnel in Iraq.

Monberg and Dragsholm. Did they meet at the hotel or what?
Yes. They did. But it was a coincidence. Monberg was at the hotel for a conference that Dragsholm also happened to

be attending. They knew each other from university days. Dragsholm, it turns out, was the love of Monberg's life. At the hotel, Dragsholm tells Monberg she has found the officer known as Perk and she wants the case into the alleged killing of civilians reopened. She also tells him the soldiers' testimonies are being disregarded.

So Monberg was having an affair with Dragsholm?

No. He was having an affair with Karina.

So why doesn't Monberg do anything about it?

Because he's leant on by Rossing. They had a secret meeting but kept no minutes. During that meeting, Rossing tells Monberg to drop legislation that would see Raben released from jail and tells him not to reopen the 3-2-Alpha case.

Why is Ruth Hedeby so determined to take Lund off the case even when she's making progress?

Higher powers may be at work. She's being leant on by Special Branch who are being leant on by Rossing. So there's that, but she's also jealous of Lund and how fond Brix is of her.

Morten Says: '*Ruth doesn't like Lund or her methods of working. Lund is far more unpredictable than a man. Men work in a direct way. Women take circles. She might mess things up but she experiences other things because of it. In Lund you have a woman who can only function when she's in the eye of the storm. And she's beating men at their own game. Ruth can't stand her. She doesn't know how to control her.*'

⋮ Sofie Says: 'There's no love lost between Hedeby and
⋮ Lund.'

✳ Fun Fact: Sofie and Ruth are best friends in real life

Who set the log trap? And who set the explosives? And what's with that weird hide?

Strange set the log trap. He also set the explosives. He left the interview with Thomsen so he had time to do it then. The hide is something that's commonly seen in woods. They're for bird-watching.

Mikael Says: 'All we did that day was laugh. We were getting closer to the hide and then when we got there it was nothing. And the pair of us were falling over in the woods. Sofie said I fell like a gazelle, very gracefully. Sofie just fell over. Because she's clumsy. She didn't look like a gazelle.'

⋮ Sofie Says: 'It's true. Mikael's nickname is now The
⋮ Embarrassed Gazelle. Every time he said "Go back to
⋮ Thomsen!" we just fell about laughing. We still say it to each
⋮ other. To this day.'

✳ Fun Fact: Mikael doesn't have a driving licence. At one point he had to drive. Sofie had to sit in the passenger seat. He drove in first gear all the way with Sofie telling him what to do. '*I was amazed I survived.*'

Why did Lund get out of the car in the forest leaving Thomsen on her own?

She is an impulsive creature and must be allowed to fly free at all times. Even if it means right royally mucking up.

Sofie Says: *'Durr. It's obvious. She thinks Strange is in danger from a shooter. And don't forget her back story of guilt – her first partner was killed in similar circumstances.'*

Why did Thomsen run away? Surely she felt safer being with the police?

She's very damaged by the war. She doesn't feel safe anywhere. She's restless and this is why she runs. Also, if she didn't run, it wouldn't be so exciting. Ssshhh.

Sofie Says: *'She's a very silly woman. And to run back to her own house? I mean please! Come on!'*

Strange must have known Thomsen would be kept in custody for her own safety and taken to Copenhagen so why did he sneak off to set explosives in her house and on her boat?

It's an excellent question. But this man covers all the bases. Remember that.

Mikael Says: *'He was doing it just in case she escaped. He was afraid that she would run off.'*

How did Strange know about Thomsen's boat anyway? She doesn't mention it in her interview.

There's a reference from the Swedish police to a mysterious call from a 'tax man' wanting to know how to find Lisbeth Thomsen. It's safe to assume that was Strange, in which case he may have already been to the island to watch her and her movements.

Mikael Says: *'Yes, there is that. But mostly, he just knows things.'* (At this point Mikael pulls a mysterious face.)

How did Strange know the code to the explosives in the depot?

He's *all over* the barracks like a virus.

Mikael Says: 'He took papers when he conducted the first search of the barracks. For him this would be easy.'

And how did he get the explosives to the island without Lund noticing?

He could have put them in the boot. He could have done that. But he didn't. Get ready, here comes the answer . . .

Mikael Says: 'He had them on his body, under his jacket.'

Wait a minute. How did Strange even know the case might be reopened? Konig, head of Special Branch, doesn't even find out till Episode 5.

Remain calm. Strange goes on his killing spree after the chance meeting with Dragsholm in the Magistrates Court. She sees his tattoo and starts asking questions. From thereon, everyone in 3–2–Alpha is doomed.

What's with this Priest guy? Is he a goody? Or a baddy? Or what?

He's a goody. But they made an oath to keep silent about the incident. Raben starts blabbing and this isn't good for anybody.

He also pretends he's never met Anne Dragsholm. Why?

Nobody wants to admit to knowing her. It's like she's the uncoolest person in the world or something.

Mikael Says: *'He's a slippery character, which is why he has to die.'*

And why, if the Priest knew about Perk, wouldn't he tell the police as soon as people started being bumped off? Is he an idiot?

It's fear. Priest's psychology runs thus: if you talk about it you're endangering your life and the lives of everyone else who was there or who knows about it. As far as all the remaining members of 3-2-Alpha are concerned, the police can't protect them.

Did Søgaard know about Perk?

He knew about the allegations that there was a rogue officer called Perk. But he had buried Per K Moller three months earlier. So he didn't believe them.

Did Søgaard know about the radio call being deleted?

No. He didn't know.

Strange is the one who tells Lund about Per K Moller. Why on earth does he do that?

Strange is trying to lay red herrings hither and thither. He has a grand scheme to stitch up Søgaard. This is merely part of his dastardly plan.

Mikael Says: *'He is really dastardly. Really, really dastardly.'*

Sofie Says: *'He is a brilliant, evil mind. He tries to mislead her and because of the Per K Moller lead she is taken off the case. He knows what he's doing.'*

How did Raben know Lund was at a wedding and where the wedding was so he could send the flowers to her?

He's sneaking round the city and watching her movements. This is the safest way he can get a message to her.

There's a nightclub above a meat-processing unit? Really?

Yes. There's an area in Copenhagen called Kødbyen (Meat City) that has meat-processing units but it has nightclubs and galleries and shops too.

Why doesn't Strange shoot Lund when he has the chance?

He fancies her. Durrrrr. Basic.

How does Raben manage to get into the officer party?

Look. They've already let someone wander in and steal explosives. Security for a party is a sad face on a stick. That's it.

Why don't Special Branch want Team Aegir or the army investigated? It's so obvious there's a military involvement.

Konig is in on the cover-up and he is coming under pressure from Rossing.

On a lighter note, isn't Strange's flat lovely?

I know. Light and bright, soft pistachio sofa, mid-height lamps. The man can arrange a room.

❋ *Fun Fact:* Strange's children are called Marcus and Clara.

What's on a number 38 Pizza?

Mikael Says: 'It's Parma ham and mushrooms, some rocket, jalapeno pepper and red pepper (with extra cheese).'

However . . .

Piv Bernth (Producer) Says: 'It's ham and mushrooms and anchovies and olives (and extra cheese).'

However . . .

Sofie Says: 'It's something with meat. A very fat sliced sausage. A castrated sausage. Loads of cheese.'

✳ *Fun Fact:* They weren't supposed to have pizza. Strange was supposed to be ordering some Japanese food. Mikael learnt Japanese specially for it and was able to say, *'I want the usual dishes but one with no wasabi.'* Lund doesn't like wasabi.

Sofie Says: 'He was rubbish at Japanese. Also there are no Japanese people in sushi restaurants in Copenhagen. (Actually he was brilliant at Japanese.)'

Who tipped off Rossing about the fax?
It was the Prime Minister. Bad business.

If he knew Raben was going to identify him, why did Strange let him see him? He could have shot him from a distance.
Strange is pretty confident that nobody is going to believe a mental patient suffering from delusions. He also knows General Arild is covering for him.

Mikael Says: 'I wish I'd shot him from the shadows. I think Strange was a bit overtired at that stage.'

So what's the deal with Captain Torben Skaning? Who is he?
They think he might be Perk. He isn't. He had a nervous breakdown (after being beasted by Søgaard for smoking dope) and was flown home with the other soldiers.

Surely Brix knew about Strange coming from Special Forces? He must have? He hired him didn't he?
Brix did hire him but no, he didn't know. Strange was forced on Brix.

Mikael Says: '*They want Brix to be the fall guy or, as they say in Denmark, he's the "guy with the monkey on the shoulder".*'

Morten Says: '*He doesn't want to believe it for the longest time. Because it would be too awful. It's astonishing he's not sacked for it, to be honest.*'

✳ *Fun Fact:* They did contemplate having Brix sacked for the Strange debacle but decided against it. Series 3 would then have started with Lund, in a mirror of the beginning of Series 2, sending for Brix, which would have been a nice touch.

Is Thomas Buch ever going to be invited back to a party at the Ministry of Integration?
No. No he isn't.

Nicolas Says: '*He might be allowed back. But only if he's on soft drinks. Having said that, we have some infamous drunks in Danish politics. There was one guy who was always pissed but he was such an amazing speaker nobody minded.*'

Why is Skopje such a terrible place to be sent?
It's not that bad. It's quite picturesque. But in diplomatic terms, it means your career is on the skids.

Nicolas Says: 'It's the exact opposite of being sent to Washington. It's the most average, boring place you can end up.'

Who is it that Buch screams 'Stop calling me, you bitch' to?
It's a journalist.

Nicolas Says: 'That bit was improvised. He's at breaking point. He's got two mobile phones, which is normal for politicians, and I wanted to show him losing it a bit.'

How did Strange activate the mobile phone in the barracks? He's in Afghanistan.
Mobile phones don't give off a signal when they're lying about, only when calls are made on them or when they are called. Strange must have made a call to it either in Afghanistan or at the airport to activate it so it sent out a signal the police could pick up.

When did he plant it there anyway?
Strange was in charge of the first search of the barracks. He did it then.

Why does Strange back Lund up when she pretends to have authorization to go to the village where the incident took place? Surely he wouldn't want her anywhere near it?
It's an odd move. He must think his placing of the dogtags

at the barracks is a surefire shoe-in for stitching up Søgaard. But he's taking a big chance here.

Mikael Says: '*He thinks he's home free and that Lund will never find the bodies. He has that psychopathic thing that people getting close slightly turns him on. He loves to watch Sarah Lund work and how her brain works. Also, he can't risk not backing her up.*'

Why do really important Danish political meetings never last longer than three minutes?

The Danes are world leaders in making decisions quickly and sticking to them.

Nicolas Says: '*This is completely normal in Denmark.*'

Oh, Bilal. Kidnapping your boss's daughter and then blowing yourself up like a suicide bomber? Really?

Yup. Given all he's done is to delete a radio message after following orders from General Arild, it does seem a tad excessive. He may have been a Muslim but he hated extremists and yet here he is, with a bomb strapped to himself, doing precisely the thing that everyone expects Muslims Who Go Bad to do.

Also, at the moment he kills himself he shouts '*For God, King and Country*', which on the face of it gives us two problems. He's a Muslim, so he doesn't follow God. He follows Allah. And Denmark doesn't have a king. It has a queen.

Mikael Says: '*This is a saying they have in Denmark so it's not literal. It's about honour. And even though suicide* *bombing is everything he hates, this is all he knows.'*

The lock-up Strange has been using as his office. Are we really supposed to believe there isn't one single speck of DNA in it? Really?

Yes. You are expected to believe that. So believe it.

Mikael Says: 'Strange always wore gloves, and a plastic hat they use in canning factories. He looked really good in that. He's a very brainy psychopath.'

So at the end of Episode 9, Raben is facing all manner of charges and is regarded as dangerous. So what in the blue blazes is he doing out and about? Shouldn't he be in custody?

Look, they let the guy wander about willy-nilly when he was in the hospital so why are we surprised he's now wandering about despite being a suspected serial killer? The Danes are terribly chilled about all this.

Also, he escapes in the montage at the end.

Buch has just told the Party top brass that he has proper evidence that the Prime Minister has ordered the cover-up of a war crime and yet they do nothing and tell Buch to just shut up about it. What's the matter with them?

If the Prime Minister falls, there'll have to be a general election and, to be honest, none of them can be bothered. Think of the paperwork.

Nicolas Says: 'To be honest, this is sort of what it was like in Danish politics for 10 years. Nobody really questioned anything.'

Raben's been shot in the arm. It seems to have improved dramatically in less than 48 hours hasn't it?

He's made of strong stuff. He's in pain. He's just not showing it.

Why didn't Plough go to the police?

Because he was convinced the Minister of Defence was behind the cover-up, but he couldn't prove it.

Morten in Series 1, Plough in Series 2 - what is it with these political assistants?

I think everyone who works in Danish politics needs to be sent on a refresher course so they can all buck their ideas up.

And as for General Arild, I mean honestly. He's bang out of order.

Yes, he is. But what are you going to do? He's under orders from the Prime Minister, he sends a Special Forces operative on a secret mission that hasn't been approved by parliament and if that gets out, everybody is going down.

So Strange has gone to a massive amount of effort to cover his tracks, pin it on Kodmani, then frame Søgaard, then Bilal. Is he really going to give the game away by casually letting slip Dragsholm was dragged across the train tracks?

Yes. I'm afraid he is.

Mikael Says: 'He had made up his mind he was going to kill Lund and he needed the excuse to do it. And he was going to jump country and carry on killing other people. If he kills her then she's his for ever. Nobody else can have her. His Sofie trophy.'

✳ **Fun Fact:** Mikael took the DVD of the last episode home to watch with his daughter, who didn't know he was the killer. At the moment he shoots Lund, she leapt from the sofa shouting, '*Oh my God! It's you! I am going to be so cool at school!*'

Nicolas Says: '*I didn't think it was going to be Strange. I had my money on Søgaard and for the longest time I had my eye on Raben. He has such a black hole inside him and was battling so many demons. But I was wrong.*'

Mikael Says: '*I was certain it was Søgaard, Bilal or Raben. I was hoping, to be honest, to be allowed to stay in and get closer to Lund, and make little police officers with jumpers. But instead I got to go off and marry the Prime Minister instead.*' (Mikael is in *Borgen*)

✳ **Fun Fact:** Sofie and Mikael were called to the Producer before Episode 8 and told that Strange was the killer.

I can't believe he shot her. But why in the chest? Wouldn't he pop her in the head?
We've been over this. He's got a soft spot for her. He doesn't want to murder her in the face.

Mikael Says: '*I did bring this up. Surely I'd just shoot her in the head? But actually, it's more in his character to shoot her through the heart and he loves her brain so he didn't want to shoot it.*'

✳ **Fun Fact:** The final showdown scene was actually shot in

August, but the series is set in November. If you look at the trees, they've all got leaves.

Sofie Says: *'A man comes whenever we have to shoot guns. Whenever he has to hand me a gun he won't let go of it. He looks at me with such mistrust. And who can blame him?'*

Was Strange lying when he tells Raben he killed the little girl first?
No. It was true. Raben started the killing.

Who is burning that photo with Strange in it at the end?
It was General Arild. CUE THE DASTARDLY MUSIC!

4

EVERYTHING YOU WILL EVER NEED TO KNOW ABOUT DENMARK

Here are all the facts you are ever going to need to pretend you are Danish. Apparently the Danish authorities are allowed to conduct spot tests on any citizen at any time, day or night, so study the following, remain vigilant and nail the anthems.

Good Luck!

DENMARK means flat land (Den) with a wooden border (Mark).

THE DANISH REALM comprises Denmark, Faroe Islands and Greenland.

FIRST MENTION IN LITERATURE: 12th century, in the *Chronicon Lethrense*. It is also referred to in the 15th-century *Ballad of Eric*.

TOTAL SURFACE AREA: 43,094 square metres

BORDER WITH GERMANY: 68 kilometres

TIDAL SHORELINE: 7,314 kilometres

NORTHERNMOST POINT:
Skagens Point, 57 45′ 7″ Northern Latitude

SOUTHERNMOST POINT:
Gedser Point, 54 33′ 35″ Northern Latitude

WESTERNMOST POINT:
Blåvandshuk, 8 4′ 22″ Eastern Longitude

EASTERNMOST POINT:
Osterskar, 15 11′ 55″ Eastern Longitude

NUMBER OF NAMED ISLANDS: 443

TOTAL NUMBER OF ISLANDS: 1,419

NUMBER OF INHABITED ISLANDS: 72

AVERAGE HEIGHT ABOVE SEA LEVEL: 102 feet

HIGHEST POINT: Møllehøoj, 560.56 feet

POPULATION: 5,475,791

LABOUR FORCE: 2.9 million

EMPLOYMENT RATE: 77.1%

TAX BURDEN (AS % OF GDP): 46%

DENMARK has the highest minimum wage in the world.

CURRENCY: Krone

DANISH DEFENCES:

Army: 15,460	Navy: 5,300
Air Force: 6,050	Danish Home Guard: 55,000

NOTABLE CONFLICTS

Northern Seven Years' War 1563 – 70 (Denmark v Sweden)

Kalmar War 1611 –13 (Denmark v Sweden)

Thirty Years' War 1618 – 48 (Denmark, Spain, Sweden, Prussia)

Siege of Copenhagen 1658 – 60 (Denmark v Sweden)

Great Northern War 1700 – 21 (Denmark and Russia v Sweden)

Napoleonic Wars 1801 and 1807 (England v Denmark)

Gunboat War 1807-1814 (England v Denmark)

Second War of Schleswig 1864 (Denmark v Prussia)

Invasion of Denmark by Germany, 9 April 1940 (Operation Weserübung). Conflict lasted for two hours before the Danish surrendered.

BICYCLE ROUTES: 12,000 kilometres

DENMARK is a constitutional monarchy and sovereign state.

CURRENT MONARCH: Queen Margrethe II

PARLIAMENTARY SOVEREIGNTY. NATIONAL LEGISLATURE: the Folketing.

MEMBERS OF PARLIAMENT: 145 elected by proportional majority plus two members each from Greenland and Faroe Islands.

CURRENT PRIME MINISTER: Helle Thorning-Schmidt

ELECTIONS: every four years

DENMARK was the first country to legalize pornography (1969).

REGISTERED PARTNERSHIPS for same-sex couples legalized in 1989.

WOMEN GIVEN THE RIGHT TO VOTE: 1915

THE DANISH FLAG is called the Dannebrog.

KONGERIGET DANMARK

DANMARK

DENMARK

Denmark has two national anthems.
Please learn both of them.

1. 'There Is A Lovely Land'

There is a lovely land
it stands with broad beeches
near the salty eastern strand

It winds itself in hill, valley,
it is called old Denmark
and it is Freja's hall.

There sat in former times,
the armour-suited warriors,
rested from conflict

Then they set out to slay the foe,
now their bones are resting
behind the mound's menhir.

That country is still lovely,
because the sea waves so blue frolic,
and the foliage stands so green

And noble women, beautiful maidens,
and men and brisk swains
inhabit the Danes' islands.

Our language is strong and soft,
Our faith is pure and purified
And courage is not dead.

And each a Danish is just free,
Each faithfully obeys his/her king,
But slavery is over.

A friendly South in the North
Is the green Dane-realm,
Your clad ax-clad Earth.

And the ship walks its proud way.
Where the plow and the keel furrows
There hope does not fail.

Our Danish flag is beautiful
The fans along the sea
With Flag Red Bay.

And always has his white colour
Your Holy Cross in blood,
O Flag of Denmark in battle.

Pure is the Danes' Spirit
It hates Prejudice's fetters,
And fascination's ties.

For friendship open, cold for mockery
Beats the Jute's honest heart,
For girl, country and king.

I swap Denmark not,
For Russia's winter deserts,
For Southern May Flowers.

We do not know plague and serpents
Not the melancholy of the west
Not the rage of the east.

Our time does not stand in reek,
It has raised his voice
Of Science and Arts.

Not Bragi's and not Mimir's cry
Aroused in equal stretch
A better hope for the future.

Not large, our native soil,
However soars among cities
Your proud Copenhagen.

To better city did the sea not come
Yes no river in the valley;
From Trondheim to Rome

With holy remand
Preserve you, All-father!
Our old dynasty.

King Fredrik resembles Fredegod
Where is a better prince
Of better hero blood?

Hail king and fatherland!
Hail every a Dane-citizen,
who works, what he can

Our old Denmark shall endure,
As long as the beech reflects
Its top in the blue wave.

2. 'King Christian Stood By The Lofty Mast'

King Christian stood by the lofty mast
In mist and smoke;
His sword was hammering so fast,
Through Gothic helm and brain it passed;
Then sank each hostile hulk and mast,
In mist and smoke.
'Fly!' shouted they, 'fly, he who can!
Who braves of Denmark's Christian,
Who braves of Denmark's Christian,
In battle?'

Niels Juel gave heed to the tempest's roar,
Now is the hour!
He hoisted his blood-red flag once more,
And smote upon the foe full sore,
And shouted loud, through the tempest's
   roar,
'Now is the hour!'
'Fly!' shouted they, 'for shelter fly!
Of Denmark's Juel who can defy,
Of Denmark's Juel who can defy,

The power?'
North Sea! A glimpse of Wessel rent
Thy murky sky!
Then champions to thine arms were sent;
Terror and Death glared where he went;
From the waves was heard a wail, that
   rent
Thy murky sky!
From Denmark thunders Tordenskiol,
Let each to Heaven commend his soul,
Let each to Heaven commend his soul,
And fly!

Path of the Dane to fame and might!
Dark-rolling wave!
Receive thy friend, who, scorning flight,
Goes to meet danger with despite,
Proudly as thou the tempest's might,
Dark-rolling wave!
And amid pleasures and alarms,
And war and victory, be thine arms,
And war and victory, be thine arms,
My grave!

Jante Law: Danish Code of Conduct

This was a concept created by writer Aksel Sandemose in his novel *A Fugitive Crosses his Tracks* (1933). His ten rules of conduct were established which place all emphasis on the collective rather than individual effort. Danish people really do follow this.

1 *Don't think you're anything special*
2 *Don't think you're as good as us*
3 *Don't think you're smarter than us*
4 *Don't convince yourself that you're better than us*
5 *Don't think you know more than us*
6 *Don't think you are more important than us*
7 *Don't think you are good at anything*
8 *Don't laugh at us*
9 *Don't think anyone cares about you*
10 *Don't think you can teach us anything*

Hygge

This is the Danish concept of cosiness. They love warmth and good cheer. It's almost indefinable but it's a sense of inner well-being as if you can bottle the feeling of sitting in front of a roaring fire wrapped in the toastiest blanket imaginable. That's *hygge*.

Great Danes

GORM THE OLD

Generally recognized as the first King of Denmark. He was married to Thyra, a woman who knuckled down and oversaw the completion of the Danevirke, a massive wall separating Denmark from its aggressive Saxon neighbour to the south. They had three sons, all of them Vikings, who set off each summer for some pillaging. One summer, one of their sons, Canute, was killed by an arrow as he sat watching some entertainments. It was seen as a ghastly act of cowardice on the part of the killer because it wasn't a fair fight. When Gorm was informed of his son's demise, he was so distraught he dropped down dead the next day. Or so they say. Before he died, however, he had a massive runestone erected – now called the Jelling Stones or Jelling Mounds.

His Jelling Stone was in memory of his wife Thyra, so perhaps she dropped down dead only moments before he did. There's no way of knowing. Anyhoo, that's the story of Gorm the Old. (Also called Gorm the Sleepy.)

HARALD BLUETOOTH

Apart from having one of the best names ever, Harald was one of the other sons of Gorm the Old and Thyra, the amazing wall-builder. He is best known for erecting the most massive of all the Jelling Stones, in memory of his parents. He had a stormy time of it during his tenure as king, was drawn into constant sticky battles with a rogue Swedish prince called Styrborn, but is credited with turning Denmark into a Christian country after his own conversion.

It's a shame his own son Swein wasn't as devoted to him as Harald had been to his parents, because in 985 Swein led a rebellion against his father during which Harald was killed.

HOLGER DANSKE
(OGIER THE DANE)

A legendary figure, Holger is supposed to have fought Charlemagne, killed a giant called Brehus and then taken up residence inside the castle Kronborg where he grew his beard down to the floor and fell asleep. According to Danish folklore he shall remain asleep until Denmark is in peril, whereupon he will wake up and save everyone and everything. He's got a massive sword called Curtana. That's it. That's all I know about him.

HAMLET

The infamous Dane that all young men with theatrical aspirations yearn to play. But let's look at the facts. A sixteen-year-old starts seeing a ghost who basically tells him to wreak revenge on all and sundry. He drives a woman to suicide, is indirectly responsible for the death of his mother, murders his new father-in-law, his father-in-law's employee, his father-in-law's son and his two best friends. He's a bloody menace.

I think it's time we all had a rethink. If Hamlet was alive today, he'd be in a very secure institution.

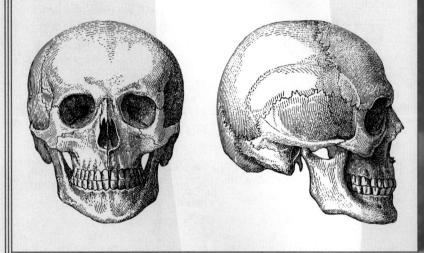

Sarah Lund wears Kathy Calmejane's winning jumper Strawberries and Crime as well as the torch and gun cosy matching set (Tine Harden)

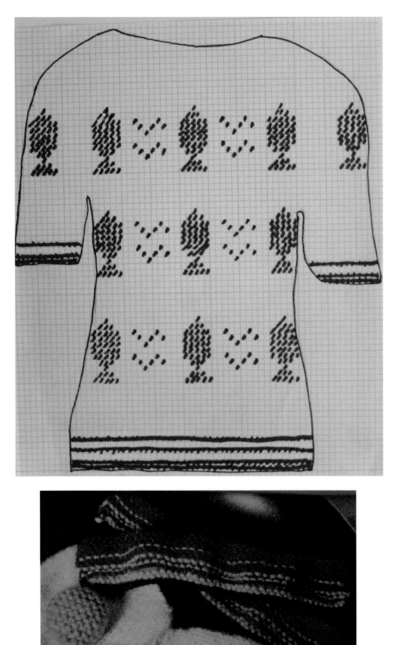

Jenny Howard took third place in *The Killing* craft competition
with her Red Herring jumper (top) and (below) the knitted
inspiration behind the streaky bacon trim (Jenny Howard)

Second place went to Lucy Squirrel with her Murder on the Dancefloor Rug (Lucy Squirrel) and the winner was Kathy Calmejane with her extraordinary Gun and Torch Cosy (Kathy Calmejane)

✳ If you're a knitter yourself, follow Kathy's patterns to knit yourself one of these (Kathy Calmejane)

Exclusive pictures of Lauren O'Farrell's Sarah Lund and killer dolls.
For more go to www.whodunnknit.com (Lauren O'Farrell)

Louisa Cudahy's brilliant Sarah Lund cross stitch (Louisa Cudahy)

TYCHO BRAHE 1546 – 1601

Tycho was an astronomer and, according to all the pictures I've seen of him, the owner of a *phenomenal* moustache. I'm cheating a bit here because he's technically from Sweden, but when he was alive he resided in Danish territory, so that'll do for me. Tycho was all about shifting celestial spheres and comets. He also came up with a geometrical/philosophical model for the universe which he rather neatly called the Tychonic System. He thought everything revolved around the Earth, which is a bit embarrassing now, but back then old Tycho was quite the man about town astronomy-wise. He was also one of the last great naked eye astronomers. Something deep within me wishes that just said naked. Let's move swiftly on.

VITUS BERING 1681 – 1741

A good old-fashioned explorer when the world was still box-fresh and nobody had been anywhere other than their own backyard. A navigator in the navy, he is primarily known for two expeditions, one along the north-east coast of Asia and the other along the west coast of America. The Bering Strait is named after him, which is a neat fact.

Sadly, he died of scurvy. He should have taken some oranges.

HANS CHRISTIAN ANDERSEN
1805 – 75

When I was seven I was taken to see Tommy Steele playing Hans Christian Andersen on stage somewhere in London. I can still sing 'Inch Worm, Inch Worm, measuring the marigolds', but enough about me and seminal theatrical experiences: Hans Christian Andersen was one of the greatest fairy-tale writers of all time. He wrote the classics *Thumbelina*, *The Little Mermaid*, *The Ugly Duckling* and, my personal favourite, *The Little Match Girl*.

Hans came to England in 1847 and was plunged into a giddy social whirl. He met Charles Dickens and stood chatting on a veranda with him and then wrote about it in his diary saying, 'I was so happy . . . I love [him] the most.' Basically Andersen had a massive man-crush on Dickens and ten years later he came back to England, just to see Dickens, managed to wangle an invite to stay at Dickens's house and then drove everyone slowly mad by staying for *five weeks*. I have seen it said that Dickens loathed Andersen and played repeated practical jokes on him. This may not be true but I suspect it is, given that he came to stay for five weeks and refused to leave despite Dickens dropping frequent hints. The upshot of his stay was that Dickens never spoke or wrote to him again. What a chump.

SØREN KIERKEGAARD 1813 – 55

Philosopher extraordinaire and brave too, given his stance on religion. Often credited as being the first existentialist philosopher, it was Kierkegaard who was the first person to stand up and say God's existence could not be proved by reason and that reason has no place in faith because God is beyond reason. According to Kierkegaard, man and man alone is responsible for giving his own life meaning.

Deeeeeeeep.

LUDWIG A. COLDING 1815 – 88

Ludwig was a physicist and a good one too, because he came up with the Principle of Conservation of Energy. Unfortunately, everyone simply ignored him. Which is a shame.

NIELS BOHR 1885 – 1962

In 1922, Niels was awarded the Nobel Prize in Physics for being utterly brainy. His particular speciality was atomic structure and quantum mechanics and he formed part of the British team working on the Manhattan Project after being secreted out of Denmark in 1943 by the Danish Resistance. Rather astonishingly, he had a son, Aage Bohr, who was *also* awarded the Nobel Prize in Physics. Not only that, but his brother, Harald, played football for Denmark. That's some family.

Asteroid 3948 Bohr is named after him.

KAREN BLIXEN 1885 – 1962

Karen, who often wrote under pen names, is best known for her stories *Out of Africa* and *Babette's Feast*, both of which have been immortalized in film. She wrote all her books in English and then translated them back into Danish.

She was an interesting character. She married a baron who gave her syphilis, divorced him and then launched herself into a lengthy love affair with a big game hunter called Denys Finch Hatton (you know, Robert Redford in the film), who was killed tragically while flying his Tiger Moth plane. Heartbroken, Karen returned to Denmark where she remained until she died in 1962. Meryl Streep was 13 years old at the time.

JØRN UTZON 1918 – 2008

Jørn is the second person in history to have a building he designed declared a World Heritage Site in his own lifetime. (The first was Oscar Niemeyer for Brasilia, which was named a World Heritage Site in 1987.) He designed the Sydney Opera House. Yeah! I know! Super impressive!

The build on the Opera was fraught with troubles, the primary one being the enormous 1,400% overspend. Utzon was in such disgrace he wasn't even invited to or even mentioned at the opening ceremony in 1973. What a shambles.

LARS ULRICH 1963 –

Well I didn't know this. Lars Ulrich, legendary drummer for hard rock gods Metallica, was actually going to be a professional tennis player. But he changed his mind and decided to do drums instead.

I expect he's glad he did. He's the first Dane ever to be inducted into the Rock and Roll Hall of Fame.

He also has a deep love of ferrets. He owns eight.

HOW TO BECOME FLUENT IN DANISH IN FIFTEEN MINUTES

The first rule, when tackling any new language, is to remain calm and tough it out. The second rule is to nod your head and say 'Tak' very loudly. Stick to these golden principles and you can pretty much fool all of the people all of the time.

Now it might seem, due to Søren Sveistrup's penchant for pared-down dialogue, that the Danish aren't that into words; but you'd be wrong. They've got loads of them.

Danish is derived from Old East Norse or Runic Danish. The Runic alphabet only had 16 letters but that didn't stop the Vikings from coming over to England and splattering the place with words that are still with us today. 'Knife', 'egg' and 'Husband', for example, are all Old East Norse words and any town ending in 'by' (Old Norse for 'town') like Whitby or Derby can safely be said to be an old Viking settlement.

So first things first. Let's start with the Danish alphabet.

A B C D E F G H I J K L M N O P
Q R S T U V W X Y Z Æ Ø Å

Yes. Well spotted. They've got three more letters than us. Twenty consonants and nine vowels, because in the land of the Danes, the Y is a vowel. Controversial.

Now, how to pronounce those letters? Here are a few handy tips.

DANISH ALPHABET	SOUNDS LIKE . . .	YOU KNOW . . .
A (a)	a	like in 'can'
Å (å)	o	like in 'oh no'
Æ (æ)	a	like in 'pay'
B (be)	b	like in 'bird'
C (se)	k	like in 'kiss'
D (de)	d	like in 'door'
E (e)	e	like in 'entrail'
F (æf)	f	like in 'fudge'
G (ge)	g	like in 'go'
H (hå)	h	like in 'help'

I (i)	e	like in 'meet'
J (jåd)	y	like in 'yes'
K (kå)	k	like in 'keeper'
L (æl)	l	like in 'love'
M (æm)	m	like in 'murder'
N (æn)	n	like in 'note'
Ø (ø)	ir	like in 'weird'
O (o)	o	like in 'old'
P (pe)	p	like in 'penalty'
S (æs)	s	like in 'sun'
T (te)	t	like in 'toe'
U (u)	o	like in 'moose'
V (ve)	v	like in 'very'
W (dobbelt-ve)	w	like in 'wobble'
X (æks)	x	like in 'axe'
Y (y)	ew	like in 'phew'
Z (sæt)	s	like in 'sun'

You might not know it but you already know *tons* of Danish. Here are just a few of the words that you can happily use in Denmark without anyone staring at you in a funny manner. Just remember to use a Danish accent when saying the Danish version and you'll be as sound as a pound. Think Swedish Chef from the Muppets, but less hairy and more Danish.

DANISH	ENGLISH
Ambulance	Ambulance
Arm	Arm
Avocado	Avocado
Babysitter	Babysitter
Bacon	Bacon
Camping	Camping
Canada	Canada
CD ROM	CD ROM
Database	Database
Denim	Denim
Email	Email
Finger	Finger
Gaffer Tape	Gaffer Tape

Hammer	Hammer
Influenza	Influenza
Internet Café	Internet Café
Jazz	Jazz
Jet Ski	Jet Ski
Jumper	Jumper
Manicure	Manicure
Melon	Melon
PDF File	PDF File
Pedicure	Pedicure
Per person	Per person
Rice	Rice
Sandal	Sandal
Sauna	Sauna
Shampoo	Shampoo
Tube	Tube
Windsurfer	Windsurfer

There. That was easy. Now let's have a go at some Danish words that are *almost* like their English cousins. Try covering up the English column and then guessing what you think the Danish word might be. This is a fun game for all the family. Get involved.

DANISH	ENGLISH
Alene	Alone
Butik	Boutique
Selleri	Celery
Krebs	Crabs
Diskotek	Discotheque
Aeg	Egg
Grapefrugt	Grapefruit
Hallo	Hello
Hjaelp	Help
Heteroseksuel	Heterosexual
Homoseksuel	Homosexual
Insekt	Insect
Midnat	Midnight
Motorbad	Motorboat
Natclub	Nightclub
Fotokopi	Photocopy

Good. Now let's get down to brass tacks. We'll start with some easy stuff and then build up to some useful phrases you'll almost certainly need on any trip to Denmark.

DANISH	ENGLISH
Tak!	Ithankyow
Hej	Hello
Hej Hej	Bye
Pis Af	Piss off
Computer (compoooooder)	Computer
For helvede	God Dang it!
Det kommer ikke dig ved	That's none of your business
Hold op	Stop it
Hvor et er natklub Boils?	Where is Boils nightclub?
Fa fingrene fra min jumper	Get your hands off my jumper
Jeg elsker bananer	I love bananas
Jeg har ingen interesse i at flytte til Sverige	I have no interest in moving to Sweden
Er du en draeber?	Are you the killer?

Good. Now let's take some of the words and phrases we've learnt and incorporate them into some utterly believable scenarios. That's right. It's *Forbrydelsen* role-play.

SCENARIO NUMBER ONE

Sarah Lund has stopped you in the street. You're a bit sweaty and confused. She's smiling at you, which is a worry.

SARAH Hej. Taler du dansk? (*Hello. Do you speak Danish?*)

YOU Ja, en smule. Computer. Email. Krebs. (*Yes, a little. Computer. Email. Crabs.*)

SARAH Hvad hedder du? (*What's your name?*)

YOU Det kommer ikke dig ved. (*That's none of your business.*)

SARAH Vil du danse med mig? (*Would you like to dance with me?*)

YOU Lad mig vaere! (*Leave me alone!*)

SARAH Jeg har haft meget travit. (*I've been very busy.*)

YOU Vil du have en cigaret? (*Would you like a cigarette?*)

SARAH Jeg er stoppet. (*I've given up.*)

(SCENE ENDS)

I think that went well. Let's try another totally plausible set-up.

SCENARIO NUMBER TWO

You've been asked to City Hall to do a PowerPoint presentation. Troels (TROOOOEELLLLLS) has met you in the corridor. He's looking shifty.

TROELS Der er blevet brudt ind i min bil. (*My car has been broken into.*)

YOU Ked af at hore det, men jeg er her for at gore en Power-Point praesentation. (*Sorry to hear that, but I'm here to do a PowerPoint presentation.*)

TROELS Tror du, at borgmesteren havde noget med det at gore? (*Do you think the Mayor had anything to do with it?*)

YOU Jeg har ingen ide. Som sagt, jeg er her for at gore en PowerPoint praesentation. (*I have no idea. Like I said I'm here to do a PowerPoint presentation.*)

RIE TROOOOOOOOOOELS! (*Troooooooooooels*)

TROELS Det er min kaereste. Hun gar gerne et tog. (*That's my girlfriend. She goes like a train.*)

YOU Det er nice (*That's nice*)

TROELS Jeg hellere ga. Ring til en pressekonference. Jeg skal aendre mit slips. (*I'd better go. Call a press conference. I am going to change my tie.*)

YOU Nej. Jeg ved faktisk ikke her. Pa den made har du en lillebitte abning. (*No. I don't work here. By the way, you have a tiny, tiny mouth.*)

(SCENE ENDS)

SCENARIO NUMBER THREE

Let's kick back a little. You're at Boils the nightclub. Oh look. It's Jens Holck.

JENS Har du faet nogen poster ved Aqua eller Whigfield? (*Have you got any records by Aqua or Whigfield?*)

YOU Jeg er ikke den DJ. (*I am not the DJ.*)

JENS Oh. Jeg troede, du ville. Pa grund af hovedtelefonerne. (*Oh. I thought you were. Because of the headphones.*)

YOU Jeg er ikke ifort hovedtelefoner. (*I'm not wearing head-phones.*)

JENS Det er svaer. (*This is awkward.*)

(SCENE ENDS)

SCENARIO NUMBER FOUR

You've got a large dining table but you don't want it any more so you decide to sell it on eBay to Pernille Birk Larsen. Let's see what happens in this thrilling yet useful encounter.

YOU Bordet er Ganske store. Du skal bruge en van. (*The table is quite large. You'll need a van.*)

PERNILLE Dette er ikke et problem. Jeg kore en fjernelse. Jeg troede, du sagde du havde set *Forbrydelsen*? (*This is not a problem. I run a removal business. I thought you said you'd seen* Forbrydelsen?)

YOU Jeg har. Hvor interessant du korer en fjernelse af van business i det virkelige liv for. (*I have. How interesting that you run a removal van business in real life too.*)

PERNILLE Ja. Der er grunden til, at jeg fik en del. (*Yes. It's why I got the part.*)

(SCENE ENDS)

SCENARIO NUMBER FIVE

You're in a bar. You're the only person in the room apart from a man. Why, it's none other than Theis Birk Larsen!

YOU Undskyld mig. Er dette saede? (*Excuse me. Is this seat taken?*)

THEIS ....
    (......................................)

YOU Hej. Beklager. Er dette saede? (*Hello. Sorry. Is this seat taken?*)

THEIS ....
    (......................................)

YOU Er du dov? Jeg vil bare vide om jeg kan sidde her? (*Are you deaf? I just want to know if I can sit here?*)

THEIS ....
    (......................................)

YOU Til helvede med dig! (*To hell with you!*)

THEIS ....
    (......................................)

(SCENE ENDS)

SCENARIO NUMBER SIX

You're walking round Copenhagen trying to find the statue of the Little Mermaid but you're quite lost. There's a man standing on the corner of the street. Hello! It's Ulrik Strange!

YOU Hej. Jeg er lost, kan du hjaelpe mig? (*Hello. I am lost can you help me?*)

STRANGE Har du faet noget smertestillende medecin? (*Have you got any painkillers?*)

YOU Hvad? Umm. Laeg roret pa. Jeg har maske et I min taske. Jeg vil bare se. Umm. Nej. Jeg har ikke. (*What? Umm. I might have one in my bag. I'll have a look. Umm. No. I haven't.*)

STRANGE Ah. (*Oh.*)

YOU Allegevel, kan du fortaelle mig, hvordan jeg skal fa den lille havfrue statue? (*Anyway, can you tell me the way to the Little Mermaid statue?*)

STRANGE Nej. (*No.*)

YOU Ah. OK. Bye. (*Oh. OK. Bye.*)

(SCENE ENDS)

SCENARIO NUMBER SEVEN

It's a lovely sunny day in Copenhagen and you're sitting in a café. Thomas Buch is at the next table.

BUCH Vil du spise disse chips? (*Are you going to eat those chips?*)

YOU De har kun lige ankommet. Jet er ikke begyndt at spise dem endnu. (*They've only just arrived. I haven't started eating them yet.*)

BUCH Ah. (*Oh.*)

YOU .... (*quietly eats a few chips*)

BUCH Er du faerdig med dem nu? (*Are you done with them now?*)

YOU Nej. Jeg har haft en stor mundfuld. Jesus! (*No. I've had one mouthful. Jesus!*)

BUCH Ah. (*Oh.*)

YOU .... (*quietly eats a few more chips*)

BUCH Hvad med nu? Det er mange chips. Jeg tror ikke du kan afslutte dem pa egen hand. (*What about now? That's a lot of chips. I don't think you can finish them on your own.*)

YOU Her er en ide. Fuck off. Fa din egen chip. (*Here's an idea. Fuck off. Get your own chips.*)

BUCH Ah. (*Oh.*)

(SCENE ENDS)

SCENARIO NUMBER EIGHT

You're enjoying a spa break on a small Danish island. You've had a game of tennis and now you'd like to get changed so you can have a swim. You walk into the changing room. Oh my goodness. Christian Søgaard is standing there.

YOU Oh my eyes! (*Oh my eyes!*)

SØGAARD Kan jeg hjaelpe dig? (*Can I help you?*)

YOU Vil du have mig til at give dem et handklaede eller noget? (*Do you want me to pass you a towel or something?*)

SØGAARD Nej. (*No.*)

YOU Ah gud. (*Oh god.*)

SØGAARD Har du kommet til fix aflob I badet? Look. Hvis jeg bojer ned kan jeg vise dig, hvor blokeringen er. (*Have you come to fix the drainage in the showers? Look. If I bend down I can show you where the blockage is.*)

YOU AH GUD. (*OH GOD.*)

SØGAARD Jeg synes det er har eller noget. (*I think it's hair or something.*)

YOU Oh, at tiden? Jeg skal ga. (*Oh is that the time? I must be going.*)

SØGAARD Jeg tror dette er showerhead browkn ogsa. Kan du give mig en handsraekning? (*I think this showerhead is broken too. Can you give me a leg up?*)

YOU Nej. Nej kan jeg ikke. Farvel. (*No. No I can't. Goodbye.*)

(SCENE ENDS)

SCENARIO NUMBER NINE

You've got a job as a part-time assistant in a men's clothing section in a Danish department store. It's been a quiet morning but, finally, you have a customer. It's Lennart Brix.

YOU Hello sir, kan jeg hjaelpe dig? (*Hello sir, can I help you?*)

BRIX Ja, jeg kunne godt taenke mig at se din mand torklaeder venligst. (*Yes. I'd like to see your range of man-scarves please.*)

YOU Helt sikkert. De er her. Hvad med denne? Den har et smukt monster. (*Certainly. They're over here. What about this one? It has a lovely pattern.*)

BRIX Nej. Jeg har faet det ene allerede. (*No. I've got that one already.*)

YOU Hvad med det bla? (*What about this blue one?*)

BRIX Jeg har faet det ene sevel. (*I've got that one as well.*)

YOU Vi har en bred vifte af gra torklaeder. (*We have a full range of grey scarves.*)

BRIX Fik dem alle. (*Got them all.*)

YOU Hvad med det rode? Med hunden pa det? Det er bare. Fra Paris. (*What about this red one? With the dog on it? It's just in. From Paris.*)

BRIX Hmmmm . . . (*Hmmmm . . .*)

YOU Jeg synes du ser super i det. (*I think you'd look super in that.*)

BRIX Ja. OK det vil jeg tage. (*Yes. OK I'll take it.*)

YOU Vil du det gave packet ind? (*Would you like it gift-wrapped?*)

BRIX Nej. Jeg onsker at baere den hjem. (*No. I want to wear it home.*)

YOU Det passer dig. (*It really suits you.*)

(SCENE ENDS)

SCENARIO NUMBER TEN

You've been arrested on suspicion of killing someone. You're in Police Headquarters. Sarah Lund is questioning you.

LUND Hvordan blev du sa vide manglenderontgenbeskriveise rontgensvar Birk Larsen? (*So how did you know Nanna Birk Larsen?*)

YOU Manglen hvad? Du har lige gjort det ord op. (*Manglen-what? You've just made that word up.*)

LUND Jeg har ikke. (*I have not.*)

YOU Er du bare en af disse online oversaettelse ting? (*Are you just using one of those online translation things?*)

LUND Nej. (*No.*)

YOU Ja du er. (*Yes you are.*)

LUND Ved ikke. (*Am not.*)

YOU Ja du ar. Nar jeg indtaster i Nanna, det koomer op manglenderontgenbeskriveise rontgensvar. (*Yes you are. When I type in Nanna, it comes up manglenderontgenbeskriveise rontgensvar.*)

LUND Aha, der er min boos stirrese gennem et to-vejs vindue. (*Oh look, there's my boss staring through a two-way window.*)

YOU Du skal ikke skifte emne. (*Don't change the subject.*)

LUND Interview over! Farvel! (*Interview over. Goodbye!*)

(SCENE ENDS)

Well done! You are now fluent in Danish. Sound as if you are being slightly sick in the back of your throat at all times and you can't go wrong.

6

DATING THE DANISH WAY AND OTHER NOBLE TRADITIONS

So you've decided you want to go Danish – but hold up. Before you sling on your best shirt, or rescue those fancy tights from the bottom of your washbag, there are a few things you're going to need to know about dating Danish-style.

Historically, the Danes don't have great provenance when it comes to romance. During their Viking period they spent most of the time raping and pillaging anyone and anything they could get their gnarly hands on but, thankfully, their wild days are firmly behind them. Courtesy and egality are now what the Danes are all about so here are the top tips you should follow if you want to get past a first date.

DON'T turn up naked. That's Swedish first dates. Easily confused, but it's the sort of fatal error your date isn't going to recover from.

DO send flowers *before* you see the object of your affections. This is expected in Danish society. Flowers should be wrapped and delivered by a flower-related professional. Not a madman dressed as a clown.

DO open any gift you may be given by your date immediately. Tossing it to the floor and forgetting about it is regarded as a terrible faux pas. Having said that, when you do open it, don't pull a face as if a horse has farted into your mouth. That's also frowned upon in Danish society.

DON'T turn your nose up at any food you are offered. You are expected to try everything, even salted licorice which the Danes are mad for but is a bona fide oral abomination. At a shove, you are allowed to refuse seconds but you will be expected to finish every last thing on your plate. Think school dinners, but with a vague chance of sex at the end of it.

DO toast your date. The Danes love this but it must be done properly. Raise your glass to eye level and say 'Skol'. The English phrase 'Up Yours' is not considered appropriate in this scenario.

DON'T behave in a raucous manner. The Danes will not stand for a Billy Loud Mouth and you may find yourself at the end of a very sharp stare or, even worse, a mild rebuke.

DON'T interrupt a Dane when they're talking. They hate it.

DON'T, whatever you do, invite yourself round to any Danish person's house. This is considered the height of impropriety. The Danish love their privacy so anyone being a Noseybonk will be quietly but firmly showed to the nearest border and asked to leave.

DON'T try and pick a fight with a Dane. They loathe

arguments and regard open expressions of feelings as a terrible weakness. If you have a tendency to get drunk on dates, poke people in the chest or cry a lot then you might want to think about dating a French or Italian person instead.

DON'T expect to be formally introduced to any of your Danish date's friends. Informality is a virtue in Denmark and you will be left to fend for yourself at any social gathering. But don't worry. You won't be expected to wrestle in a leotard. Much.

Sofie Says: 'You can't get a date with Sarah Lund. The only way to get near her is to attack her somehow. You have to make a surprise manoeuvre. Pretend you fall on her. That would be a good beginning.'

Other Noble Danish Traditions

It's very important, when in Denmark, that you muck in when it comes to traditional festivals. Nobody likes a party pooper, unless you're Sarah Lund, in which case *all* Danish traditional festivals are for turning up, looking awkward, and then leaving. All the same, you still need to know the form. So here are the main Danish knees-ups and their protocols.

SHROVETIDE

This is held on Quinquagesima or 'Pork' Sunday. No. I don't know what that is either. Danish children dress up in costumes and go door to door with collection tins begging for money. To get the money, they have to ring a bell and sing the following song:

> '*Boller op, boller ned, boller i min mave,*
> *hvis jeg ingen boller får, så laver jeg ballade*
>
> ('*Buns up, buns down, buns in my tummy,*
> *If I don't get any buns, I'll make trouble*')

In other words, they mean business. Best advice is to cough up the Kroner instantly, no questions asked. It may seem like they want buns. But they don't. They want cold, hard cash.

Shrovetide rods, usually birch branches covered with sweets or presents, can be given to the children to fend off their insatiable desire for buns, but stick to money and you can't go wrong.

During Shrovetide, children, as well as extorting cash from strangers, will also 'Tilt at the cat in the barrel' – in other words, they smash a suspended barrel filled with sweets with clubs. The most violent child (first to knock a hole in the barrel) becomes the King or Queen of Cats.

According to suspicious Danes, the cat is the companion of witches and demons and therefore evil; and until the mid 19th century, Danes would fend off bad luck by placing a live cat in a barrel which was then beaten until the cat ran away when the barrel broke. True life.

SAINT HANS DAY

This is held on 23 June.

Clearly, the Danes are terrified of witches because this

summer solstice tradition is all about warding off evil spirits. Bonfires are lit, a song, 'Vi elsker vort land' ('We love our country') is sung and an effigy of a witch is burnt. Mostly, it's a celebration of Danish cosiness, a concept dear to the Danes' hearts. However, don't be confused. Grabbing old women and throwing them onto fires is generally frowned upon in modern Danish society, so when invited to 'make yourself cosy' don't make that mistake. Like I did. Awkward.

VALDEMAR'S DAY
King Valdemar II was the King of Denmark from 1202 to 1241. He's also know as Valdemar the Victorious, given his predilection for invading places willy-nilly and conquering them. According to legend, when Valdemar was on one of his conquering sprees in Estonia, the Danish flag (Dannebrog), fell from the sky. I'm sceptical but if that's what they're telling us, then so be it. Since 1913, Valdemar's day is a day when small Danish flags are sold and then waved.

That's it.

MARTINMAS EVE
Simply an excuse to eat roast goose stuffed with prunes. Get stuck in.

CHRISTMAS
Now you might think, how different can this be? Well. Get ready because Christmas in Denmark is *quite* different.

It's controversial, but in Denmark they open their presents on *Christmas Eve*. Yeah. They light candles, walk hand in hand around the Christmas tree singing songs and then they open their presents. The scamps.

Christmas Day is more like ours but they don't eat turkey. They don't go near the stuff. Instead they have either roast duck or roast pork. And they serve it with sugar potatoes. You boil some potatoes and then you put them in a pan with brown sugar and butter and caramelize them.

Then for pudding (the Danes don't have figgy pudding) they have 'ris a la mande' – rice pudding with almonds. And instead of finding the penny in the pudding, the Danes pudding game is who gets the Mandelgave – the almond gift. There's a whole almond somewhere in the 'ris a la mande'. But they're sticklers for rules: if you find the 'Mandelgaven', you have to keep it secret until everyone has eaten their portion. You can find the recipe for Risalamande in Chapter 9.

Glogg is the Danes' Christmas drink. It's basically mulled wine but has a brilliant name so is, therefore, loads better.

The Julefrokost is a pre-Christmas lunch with friends and colleagues. Rye bread and herring, pickles and meats are eaten and it's all washed down with schnapps and beer. So it's like our Work Do but with more finger snacks.

NEW YEAR'S EVE

Marzipan ring cake is served at midnight. Good-luck meals of boiled cod, stewed kale and pork are eaten and people get dishes of food and leave or smash them on the threshold of friends' and families' houses. What a mess. And then they all get rat-arsed. Just like us.

BIRTHDAYS

Now, what to do if it's someone's birthday? We get a clue in *The Killing* in Episode 1 of Series 2 because Sarah Lund has to go to a birthday party. The Danes have a traditional song they like to sing at birthdays. They also like to wave the Dannebrog in the face of the person whose birthday it is. Then, like us, they eat cake. Traditional birthday cake is called Lagkage. It's usually a soft sponge and can have a variety of fillings, but the top must be iced and covered in Danish flags and candles.

It is very important to remember that as soon as you've sung the song and handed over an unsuitable present, you then leave immediately because you've developed a sudden obsession with cellophane.

Explain nothing.

And there it is. Those are the main Danish traditions you may have to deal with.

Skol!

7

DANISH POLITICS (THE BRAINY BIT)

In the world of *The Killing* there are two political arenas:

1. City Hall
2. Parliament

The former is the home of the Mayor of Copenhagen and all the local politicians who spend their time fretting about integration projects, housing issues and playing basketball. The latter is where the big boys and girls jostle position and bang chests over matters of national importance like whether or not to assist in a massive cover-up involving wartime atrocities. That sort of thing.

City Hall has large sweeping staircases and cavernous corridors. Offices are clad with dark wood and terribly lit. This is why just about everybody has to wear glasses. Parliament, on the other hand, is considerably brighter, has more efficient heating (everyone's in shirtsleeves) and has specially built meeting rooms where politicians are allowed to gather but *only* if they've torn a massive page out of their own moral compass handbook and are prepared to do the shadowy Prime Minister's bidding.

Leather sofas are terribly popular, as are low-slung coffee

City Hall

Parliament

tables and Anglepoise lamps that cast nothing but the dim beam of suspicion.

One thing binds the two buildings. In Danish politics, whatever the level, no one party is ever really in charge. There can be a majority party but they won't have enough of a majority to do anything. This means they have to form constant coalitions with whoever they can get their hands on which, in turn, leads to endless meetings in dim rooms where haggling over nutty policy points lasts for precisely three minutes (it can never be longer, they put an egg timer on just to make sure). Basically, whoever speaks last before the egg timer goes off wins. That's it.

The other major Danish negotiation practice is to hastily call a press conference. In Denmark, journalists and their photographers are required to stand in corridors just outside any politician's office at all times and be ready the nanosecond they're called. The press conference begins as soon as the minister opens his office door and ends as soon as he pulls a face that suggests he can't quite remember why he called the press conference in the first place *or* he has lower abdominal pain.

You might think that Danish journalists are sick and tired of having to constantly stand about waiting for minor pronouncements, but you'd be wrong. Danish politicians provide the greatest scandals imaginable:

Mayoral candidate number one suspect in murder case

Mayoral candidate arrested for murder

Mayoral candidate released, gives Mayor heart attack, becomes Mayor two days later.

What this tells us is that Danish voters will still vote for someone tarred with the shitty stick of scandal day in day out for the 19 days running up to an election. Amazing. They're an independent bunch.

Something else you may like to know about Danish politics is that everyone is allowed to smoke. Even children. And dogs. In Denmark, they haven't quite realized yet that smoking is bad for you, apart from Sarah Lund, who *has* realized it and has successfully incorporated chewing nicotine gum into her thinking time.

The gum-chewing is, of course, essential given the massive amount of thinking Sarah Lund is forced to do. For reasons best known to themselves, the powers that be at Police Headquarters have decided a massive murder investigation involving a serial killer and bodies dropping left right and centre should be assigned to just two police officers. Mind you, Denmark is quite a small country. There are only five million suspects. It's a walk in the park.

Backstabbing is de rigueur. Despite Denmark being officially the least corrupt nation in the world, dirty tricks still occur and affairs are not only commonplace but expected. For this reason, Party flats are essential. In the world of *The Killing*, Party flats are used for three things and three things only:

1. Getting drunk in whilst in a terribly maudlin state
2. Internet dating
3. Having sex with Nanna Birk Larsen

Interestingly, parliament politicians do not have Party flats. Instead, they're expected to sleep in their offices, which is all very well but some cotton-headed ninny muggin forgot to put sinks in. Teeth are cleaned in glasses of schnapps. It's the Danish way and, in case you're wondering, hotels are where Danish parliamentarians go for their playing away sexy time. Old school. Nice.

Every Danish politician, whether local or national, is required to appear on television in a debate hosted by someone who has been physically restrained from combing their hair and is medically prevented from expressing any facial emotions. Bar stools and glass tables seem to be the furniture of choice, whilst backdrops include windbreaks hauled out of the back of a skip. It is very, very important during Danish political television debates that everybody, but everybody, looks utterly livid as if they all know they've got tickets to the theatre but have no chance of getting there.

Second-in-commands play a vital role in all aspects of Danish politics. Posts are highly sought-after and years of training have to be undertaken before you can even be considered for the job of right-hand man. Responsibilities include:

1. Withholding vital evidence
2. Always carrying a sponge for blood wipe-down emergencies
3. Sneaking inflammatory memos into files
4. Plain bare-faced lying
5. Perfecting the wet-lipped wounded look when your boss inevitably turns on you in an act of self-preservation

Remember, they make it look easy because they're good at it. Do not try this at home.

If you want to be a politician's mistress then there are a couple of things you need to tuck under your belt. It's easy and convenient to think *you* are *his* biggest secret. You're not. Not by a long chalk. Prepare yourself for bombshells along the lines of, *'You know how you thought I was really happy? I wasn't. I miss my wife. So I drove drunk halfway across Denmark to stick my head in an oven'*, and *'I am now going to kill myself because the woman I loved twenty years ago has been stabbed 21 times'*.

There's a theme here. In other words, whoever you are and whichever politician you've chosen, he simply loves someone else more. And that someone else is *dead* so you can't even scratch her eyes out.

Politics sucks.

✳ ◌ ✳ ◌ ✳ 8 ✳ ◌ ✳ ◌ ✳

GET THE LOOK –
DANISH INTERIOR DESIGN

Hey you! You're a hip, young, urban thingabouttown. You like clean lines with a minimalist appeal. You've got yourself a flat and you want to go Danish.

STOP. STOP WHAT YOU ARE DOING. GET OUT OF YOUR CAR. IKEA IS NOT DANISH. THAT'S SWEDEN. And relax. You've just saved yourself an hour and a half arguing on the North Circular, stocking up on utterly pointless nicknacks you don't need but seem brilliant at the time simply because they're called 'Bork' or 'Knooob' and gorging on meatballs.

Step away from the madness.

If you want the beautiful, restrained elegance of a Danish interior then here are the four essentials that are your new must-haves:

1. Moulded seats that mimic body shape

2. Furniture made from oak or teak steam-bent into shape. Yes. I said steam-bent. Sexy.

3. **Clean lines.** *If you've got a set of drawers, it needs no inlaid wood or fancy patterns. Let the wood be wood. And if you've got something that needs a furnishing, it's wool, leather or nothing.*

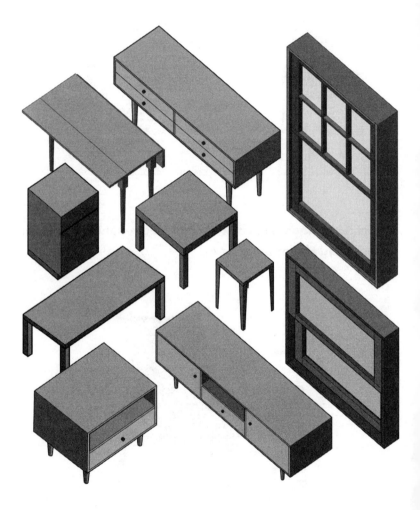

4. Brightly coloured plastics and tubular metal framework

Danish interior design is the furniture equivalent of the little black dress. It's *always* going to look cool, sleek and create that laid-back atmosphere that says '*Yeah, I'm Danish, look impressed.*' Relaxing yet spacious, that's the vibe that's going down. It says kick off your shoes, let your hair down and undo a jar of pickled herrings.

Natural colours and elements are now your best friend. Neutral tones are a must and wall-lighting is essential for that uncluttered look.

Low coffee tables (wood or glass) are never frowned upon and windows should remain uncovered. The Danes love their light. Let it in.

Bold, abstract art may be placed on walls. If you must have nicknacks, keep them to a minimum, keep them ceramic and present them on glass shelves.

A wool rug is acceptable. Just.

Plants are fine, but keep them to a minimum. You're not living in a greenhouse.

Danes don't understand carpet, so don't try and bamboozle them with a flock pile. Bare wooden floors are a must. Thank you.

You'll need a bed. You want teak, or walnut with features such as bedside shelves and night lights incorporated into the frame. Yes. That's a thing that exists. It's not just some utopian dream.

Versatile and sturdy. That's the gift your Danish sofa is never going to stop giving. Crisp lines and angles allow for maximum functionality. Sit on it. Lie on it. Do handstands on it. It's up to you. There's no *end* to what you can do on your sofa.

Dining table? Corner table? Occasional table? *No* worries. The Danes have got them covered. Simple, gorgeous, meticulously crafted, your Danish table is everything you will ever want from a table. It's so table-y. So practical! So wipe-down. Mmmm. Table.

Well done. You should by now have achieved the perfect marriage between form and function.

So take your fucking shoes off.

9

DANISH RECIPES

The Danes are pork-mad. They love pork. They can't get enough of it. In fact Denmark has the highest per capita consumption of pork in the world. The reason? Danish food has its roots back, through the mists of time, in the peasant dishes that were family staples pre-Industrial Revolution. In a nutshell, the only things they had to eat were the things they had on the farm, so bread, potatoes and salted pork were the daily staples.

But that was then and this is now. So let's have a look at a typical day's food for the Danes. Clearly there is no point in providing Sarah Lund's typical day's food because all that would be is one sadly fried egg and a packet of nicotine gum.

BREAKFAST

Danes like to start their days with a slice of rye bread and a bit of cheese and jam. Yes. You read correctly. Cheese *and* jam. I've seen it with my own nekkid eyes. It's seven shades of wrong. Cold meats may also make an appearance. Think a British lunch but for breakfast and with inappropriate jam use. They also, very kindly, invented Wienerbrød – Danish pastries to you and me – for which the world must give never-ending thanks.

If you want to experience a deeper, braver cut when it comes to breakfast, then why not try Øllebrød – a porridge made from rye bread and dark beer. Here's how you make it. This will serve four.

500 g dark rye bread, cut into pieces
1 litre water
170 ml dark beer (you can use alcohol-free if you like)
2 egg yolks
100 g caster sugar
whipped cream or chopped fruits, to serve (optional)

Place the rye bread in a bowl with the water. Cover, and leave to soak for a few hours. Transfer the soaked bread to a saucepan, place it over a medium heat and boil the mixture until it becomes an even paste, then simmer for 15 minutes. Add the beer. Whip egg yolks and sugar together until pale and creamy and add just before serving. You can add whipped cream or chopped fruits depending on personal taste.

LUNCH

It's all about the Smørrebrød: Rye bread with a topping of cold meat, or pickled herring, or cheese, or egg, or liver paste with (and this is the controversial bit) no other piece of rye bread to finish it off on top. It's the classic unfinished sandwich. The Danes are mad for it. You can make your own liver paste if you like. Here's a recipe.

450 g pork liver
3 anchovy fillets
280 g pork fat or lard
1 onion
30 g plain flour
60ml single cream
2 medium/large eggs
2 teaspoons salt
1 teaspoon ground black pepper
¼ teaspoon allspice

Put the liver, anchovy fillets, fat or lard and onion in a food processor and blend till smooth. Transfer to a bowl and mix in the flour, cream, eggs, salt, pepper and allspice. Pour the mixture into a buttered loaf tin. (If you want it to be silky smooth then pass it through a sieve first.) Place the loaf tin in a bain-marie and bake in a 180°C oven for an hour. If you don't want the top to go brown, put foil over the top as it cooks.

DINNER

Dinner is, rather confusingly, often called Middag (Midday) and will invariably be a bit of meat (usually pork) with potatoes and a vegetable. Some wilder Danes might serve a salad. Meatballs, yellow split pea soup, ground beef steak and onions, fried pork and parsley sauce, poached cod, smoked eel – all of these are typical Danish suppers.

Aebleflaesk is a particular favourite – it's sautéed belly of pork with apple. And here's how you make it.

Belly of boneless, salted pork joint, cut into slices
1 tbsp oil, for frying
4 apples, cut into rings peeled, cored and sliced
70 g caster sugar

Shallow-fry slices of lightly salted pork belly in oil. When crispy, remove from the pan and set aside.

In the same pan and without cleaning it, fry the apple rings. Sprinkle with sugar and allow to caramelize. Serve with roasted, boiled or mashed potatoes and gravy.

Sofie Says: *'I have an amazing Lund recipe. It's called Fried Egg. I take an egg and a pan. And I heat the pan till it's quite hot. And then I crack the egg with a knife, away from the pan, and then I whisk the egg with a fork in a bowl. Oh wait. That's scrambled egg.'*

PUDDING

The Danes tend not to have pudding unless it's a special occasion or they're eating out. But two very popular ones are Rødgrød med Fløde and the Christmas traditional pudding Risalamande. Because I am spoiling you, here are recipes for both.

Rødgrød med Fløde

600 g fresh raspberries
400 g fresh strawberries, hulled
150 g granulated sugar
70 g corn starch

120 ml water
60 ml double cream
2 teaspoons icing sugar
¼ teaspoon vanilla extract
180 ml Greek yogurt

Place the raspberries and strawberries in a food processor and blend until smooth. Pass through a sieve into a saucepan, to remove pips. Add the granulated sugar. Whisk the corn starch and water together in a bowl and add the berry mix. Cook over a medium heat, whisking constantly until the sugar has dissolved and the mixture starts to bubble and thicken.

Allow it to cool, cover in cling film and chill for two hours. The cling film prevents a crust forming. The mixture will thicken as it cools.

Whip the cream to soft peaks. Add the icing sugar and vanilla extract then whip until firm peaks form. Fold in the yogurt.

Serve the pudding with a dollop of vanilla cream on top.

Risalamande

½ litre full fat milk
140 g rice
400 ml cherry juice
2 teaspoons corn starch
40 g preserved cherries
25 g almonds
240 ml single cream whisked to soft peaks
1 teaspoon vanilla essence
1 tablespoon caster sugar

Pour the milk into a saucepan and simmer gently over a low heat. Add the rice. Stir continuously but gently and cook over a low heat for 45 minutes. When the rice is tender, let it cool.

Bring the cherry juice to a simmer. Mix the corn starch with a little cold water. Take a ladle of the cherry juice and add it to the corn starch mix, whisking constantly. When mixed, add the corn starch mix to the saucepan of cherry juice, along with the vanilla and sugar, and whisk. Add the cherries. Cook further so that the corn starch thickens the sauce.

Chop the almonds and mix into the rice pudding. Then add the whisked cream.

Serve the rice pudding cold with cherry sauce poured over the top.

✖✖✖ 10 ✖✖✖

THE KILLING
CRAFT CORNER

The single most important thing you are going to need on your quest to become Sarah Lund is the Jumper.

If you want to buy the original Series 1 and Series 2 Jumpers then you can. They're made by Gudrun & Gudrun and are available for sale online at their website www.shop. gudrungudrun.com/

But perhaps you're a knitter. Perhaps you want to have a go at creating your *own* Jumper? Well now you can. Here, then, are our homage knitting patterns. Get stitching.

Sarah's White Jumper
by Kathy Calmejane, inspired by the original design by Gudrun & Gudrun

Sizes:
S (M, L, XL, XXL) – Note: These jumpers are designed to be close-fitting. If you'd like a looser fit, pick the next size up.

Recommended yarn:
Origin' Merinos (Bergère de France)

SARAH'S WHITE JUMPER
by Kathy Calmejane
Finished sizes (after blocking) – all measurements in cm

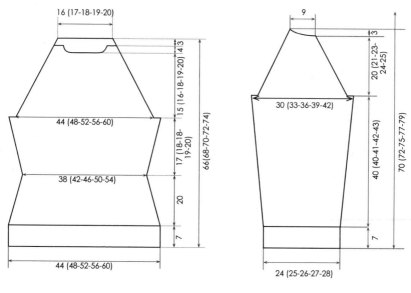

Front/back

Sleeves

Fair-isle pattern chart

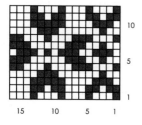

☐ 1 stitch in base colour

■ 1 stitch in accent colour

Colours:

Cocon (white) – 8 (8, 10, 10, 11) x 50g skeins – 840 m / 918
    yrds (840/918, 1050/1147, 1050/1147, 1155/1252)
Fougue (black) – 2 (2, 3, 3, 3) 50g skeins – 110 m / 230 yrds
    (110/230, 315/344, 315/344, 315/344)

Base colours for other jumper colours in same yarn (use Cocon/white as the accent colour):

Brasier (brown)
Etreinte (navy blue)

Gauge/swatch:

10 cm / 4″ = 16 sts x 25 rows

Needles:

A pair of 5 mm needles[1] + 5.5 mm circular needles (40–60
cm length)

Note:

As this pattern caters for several colour combinations, it will
refer to 'base' and 'accent' colours rather than white and
black respectively.

BACK

1. Using straight needles, cast on 70 (78-82-90-98) sts.
   Next row: k2, p2, repeat until end of row, k2.
2. Continue working sts as they come until you have a
   total of 18 rows (7 cm).
3. Knit next row, and continue working in stockinette st.
4. After 4 rows stockinette, begin first decrease row: k2,
   k2tog, knit until end of row, ssk, k2. Repeat this decrease
   row every 8 (8-12-8-6) rows, repeating 5 (6-4-5-6)
   times in total.

5. *At the same time*, begin chart on row 11 of the stockinette (row 29 total): k1 then start with stitch 10 (6-4-1-13) of chart and repeat until 1 st remains, k1[2]. Continue pattern until top of chart (while continuing to decrease as above) then continue in stockinette in base colour.

6. At 27 cm (68 rows) total, begin first increase row: k2, inc 1, knit until 2 sts remain, inc 1, k2.

7. Repeat this increase row every 6 (6-8-6-6) rows, repeating 5 (6-4-5-6) times in total.

8. *At the same time*, at 33 cm (78 rows) total, RS facing you, k1 then begin pattern chart on stitch 13 (9-5-3-16) and repeat until 1 st remains, k1 in base colour. Continue pattern until top of chart then continue in stockinette in base colour.

9. At 44 cm total, RS facing, begin the raglan[3] by binding off 2st at beg of next 2 rows.

10. Decrease row (RS): k2, ssk, knit until 3 sts remain, k2tog, k1, repeat every 2 rows, 18 (23-25-26-31) times in total.

11. *At the same time*, and continuing decreases as above, on row 11 from beginning of raglan, RS facing you, k1 then begin pattern chart on stitch 1 (13-10-5-16) and repeat until 1 st remains, k1.

12. After all the decreases have been made, work straight until raglan is 22 (23-25-26-27) cm high, then cast off remaining 26 (27-28-30-32) stitches.

FRONT

1. Repeat steps 1 – 9 of instructions for back.

2. Decrease row (RS): k2, ssk, knit until 3 sts remain, k2tog, k1, repeat 2 rows, 16 (21-23-24-29) times.

3. *At the same time*, while continuing the raglan decreases, begin the neckline:
   a. When raglan is 15 (16-18-19-20) cm high, k14 and place those stitches on stitch holder.
   b. Bind off central 10 (12-12-14-16) sts, then knit to end.
   c. Decrease at neck edge every 2 rows: 3, 2, 2, 1 sts.
   d. Pick up stitches on holder and repeat step c for the other side of the neckline.
   d. Pick up stitches on holder and repeat step c for the other side of the neckline.
4. Bind off remaining 4 sts. Repeat steps 10 and 11 for stitches on holder.

SLEEVES (MAKE TWO)

1. Cast on 38 (42-42-42-48) sts and *k2, p2*, repeat * to * until 2 sts remain, k2.
2. Continue working sts as they appear until sleeve is 7 cm long (18 rows)
3. Row 19: knit all stitches and continue in stockinette.
4. Count 6 rows from top of cuff, on RS: (Increase row) k2, inc1, knit until 2 sts remain, inc. 1, k2.
5. Repeat increase row 5 (6-8-10-11) times in total, every 18 (16-12-10-8) rows.
6. At the same time: 4 rows after top of cuff, begin pattern chart starting at stitch 9 (7-7-7-6).
7. *While continuing increases*, begin pattern chart again 24 (24-26-26-26) plain rows after end of first pattern starting at stitch 7 (4-3-3-1), RS facing.
8. *While continuing increases*, begin pattern chart again 24 (24-26-26-26) plain rows after end of second pattern starting at stitch 5 (2-16-15-13), RS facing.

9. Begin raglan at 47 (47-48-49-50) cm total length, bind off 2 st at beginning of next 2 rows to begin the sleeve cap.

10. Decrease row (RS): k2, ssk, knit until 3 sts remain, k2tog, k1. Repeat this row every 4 rows, 10 (7-7-4-1) times in total, then every 2 rows 4 (10-12-17-23) times in total.

11. *While continuing decreases*, 12 rows after beginning of raglan, begin pattern chart at stitch 9 (5-4-3-16).

12. Neckline: bind off the following numbers of stitches at the beginning of the next rows, starting on the next RS after the last decrease row: 4, 1, 3, 1, 2, 0, 2, 0, then bind off the remaining 3 sts. When making the other sleeve, bind off as follows: 1, 4, 1, 3, 0, 2, 0, 2 then the remaining 3 sts.

COLLAR

1. Cast on 88 (92-96-100-104) sts on circular needles. Knit in 2-2 rib in the round (k2, p2) until collar is 6 cm high.

2. Change to a contrasting colour yarn and cast off. This cast off will be unravelled when assembling so use a yarn that will be easy to pull out. Leave a long tail of base colour yarn when changing, so that it can be used to assemble collar.

FINISHING

1. Block to measurements on chart. This step is important as it will relax the yarn, especially in the fair-isle pattern sections and allow you to check that your jumper will fit correctly. Allow all sections to cool and dry completely before assembling.

2. Sew raglan seams, using either a backstitch or invisible/ mattress stitch.

3. Sew sleeve seams and side seams, using either a backstitch or invisible/mattress stitch.
4. To assemble collar, thread your needle with the tail of base colour yarn from the collar and begin undoing contrasting cast-off one stitch at a time. Alternately slip your sewing needle into the neckline of the main body and through the stitches of the collar as they become free from the cast-off yarn.
5. Secure and weave in all ends.

Footnotes

1. Knitting fair-isle is very much a question of tension and this jumper should be knit at a regular, medium tension and fit quite snugly at first, as the yarn will relax a little with use and washing. For a looser fit, or if you tend to knit quite tight, switch to 5.5 mm needles when doing the pattern sections.
2. For all pattern rows, the stitch indicated to start with will always be worked on the 2nd stitch of your row. For a nice, regular edge, always leave the first and last stitch of every row 'plain', in the base colour. This will make assembling easier. When starting or ending a colour pattern section, knit the first stitch with both yarns together to secure the end.
3. To make it easier to measure the height of the raglan, take a length of contrasting yarn and thread it through the stitches of the first row in step 8. This will allow you to take a straight measurement in the middle of the work. Don't forget to remove the contrasting yarn before assembling!

Sarah's Red Jumper

by Kathy Calmejane, inspired by the original design by Gudrun & Gudrun

Sizes:

S (M, L, XL, XXL)

Recommended yarn:

Norvège (Bergère de France)

Colours:

Viking (red) - 8 (10-10-11-12) x 50g skeins - 1120 m / 1224 yrds (1400 / 1530 - 1400 / 1530 - 1540 / 1683 - 1680 / 1836)

Gauge/swatch:

10 cm of stockinette = 20 sts x 26 rows

Needles:

4 mm knitting needles + 5 mm circular needles (40 – 60 cm length)

SARAH'S RED JUMPER
by Kathy Calmejane
Finished sizes (after blocking) – all measurements in cm

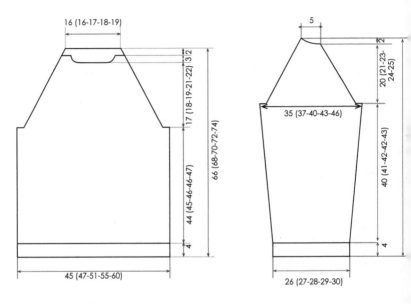

Front/back

Sleeves

Pattern chart

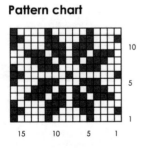

□ knit stitch on Right Side
■ perl stitch on Right Side

BACK

1. Cast on 90 (94-102-110-118) stitches on straight needles.
2. Knit in 2-2 rib (k2, p2) until ribbing is 10 rows (4 cm) high.
3. Knit all next row, purl all following row, and continue straight in stockinette until back is 48 (49-50-50-51) cm total length - 124 (128-130-130-132) rows total.
4. Begin raglan by binding off 1 (1-2-3-5) sts at beginning of next 2 rows.
5. Decrease row (RS): k2, ssk, knit until 3 sts remain, k2tog, k1. Repeat this row every RS row 28 (30-32-34-34) times in total.
6. *At the same time*, on the 7th row from the start of raglan, on RS, begin knitting the chart on stitch 11 (10-5-1-14) and repeat until end of row. Work in pattern until you reach the top of the chart (12 rows).
7. Once all decreases have been made, cast off the 32 (32-34-36-38) remaining stitches at 22 (23-24-26-27) cm or 58 (62-66-72-72) rows from beginning of raglan.

FRONT

1. Repeat steps 1 to 4 of instructions for back.
2. Decrease row (RS): k2, ssk, knit until 3 sts remain, k2tog, k1. Repeat this row 17 (27-29-31-31) times.
3. *At the same time*, on the 7th row from the start of raglan, begin knitting in pattern on RS, begin chart on stitch 11 (10-5-1-14) and repeat until end of row. Work in pattern until you reach the top of the chart (12 rows).

4. *While continuing decreases* on the raglan side, at 17 (18-19-19-21-22) cm from start of raglan, when 42 (42-42-44-46) sts remain, begin the neckline as follows:

5. k13 sts and place on stitch holder. Bind off 16 (16-16-18-20) sts. Work remaining 13 sts to end of row.

6. Work next row as it comes.

7. Bind off 4 sts at neckline side and work to end of row. Work next as it comes.

8. Bind off 2 sts at neckline side and work to end of row. Work next as it comes.

9. Bind off 2 sts at neckline side and work to end of row. Work next as it comes.

10. Bind off remaining sts.

11. Pick up stitches from holder and work steps b to f above to form other side of neckline.

SLEEVES (MAKE TWO)

1. Cast on 54 (54-58-58-62) sts on straight needles.

2. Knit in 2-2 rib (k2, p2) until cuff is 10 rows (4 cm) high.

3. Beginning on RS, work 8 rows of stockinette.

4. Increase row (on RS): k2, inc 1, knit until 2 sts remain, inc 1, k2. Repeat this row a total of 8 (10-11-14-15) times, every 10 (8-8-6-6) rows.

5. At 44 (45-46-46-47) cm total length or 114 (118-120-120-122) rows, begin raglan by binding off 4 sts at beginning of next 2 rows, then 2 sts at the beginning of the next 2 (2-8-8-10) rows.

6. Decrease row (RS): k2, k2tog, knit until 3 sts remain, ssk, k1. Repeat this row every RS row 24 (26-24-26-27) times.

7. *At the same time while continuing decreases*, on the 7th

row from the start of raglan, on RS, begin knitting the chart on stitch 8 (4-3-1-13) and repeat until end of row. Work in pattern until you reach the top of the chart (12 rows).

8. After last decrease row, bind off at the beginning of following rows: 4, 0, 3, 0 then final 3 sts. When making second sleeve, bind off in the following order: 0, 4, 0, 3, 0 the final 3 sts.

COLLAR

1. Cast on 88 (92-96-100-104) sts on circular needles and knit in the round: *k2, p2* repeat * to * until collar is 4 cm high (10 rows).

2. Change to a contrasting colour yarn and cast off. This cast off will be unravelled when assembling so use a yarn that will be easy to pull out. Leave a long tail of base colour yarn when changing, so that it can be used to assemble collar.

   Alternative for straight 5 mm needles: Cast on 2 more sts than indicated above and knit as above ending with an extra k2 at the end of first line. Knit double ribbing until piece is 4 cm long, then cast off with contrasting yarn as above. When assembling, sew the 2 short ends together first then assemble as directed.

FINISHING

1. Block to measurements on chart. This step is important as it will relax the yarn and allow you to check that your jumper will fit correctly. Allow all sections to cool and dry completely before assembling.

2. Sew raglan seams, using either a backstitch or invisible/mattress stitch.
3. Sew sleeve seams and side seams, using either a backstitch or invisible/mattress stitch.
4. To assemble collar, thread your needle with the tail of base colour yarn from the collar and begin undoing contrasting bind-off 1 st at a time. Alternately slip your sewing needle into the neckline of the main body and through the stitches of the collar as they become free from the bind-off yarn.
5. Secure and weave in all ends.

So that's the Jumpers sorted. But perhaps you want to make your very own Little Knitted Sarah Lund? The very brilliant Lauren O'Farrell, otherwise known as @deadlyknitshade, the knitting graffiti artist, has designed a Sarah Lund doll and a killer doll. She's very kindly allowed me to reproduce her patterns here. You can check out her website www.whodunnknit.com, which is packed with great stuff and has information on all the brilliant knitting books she's written.

Little Knitted Sarah Lund
by Lauren O'Farrelll otherwise know as @deadlyknitshade

Little Knitted Sarah is a hard-working, jumper-wearing, tenacious detective lady. She's made from yarn but that doesn't mean she's soft and squishy, oh no. She'll unravel the mystery of the murder even if it means no sleep for a week and wearing 'that Jumper' the whole time, and she won't move to Sweden until she does.

Size:
Approximately 17 cm

Gauge:
Not important

Recommended yarns:
8g Light pink DK yarn (skin)
8g Cream DK yarn (jumper)
5g Blue DK yarn (jeans)
Small amount Black DK yarn (pattern)
5g Dark brown DK (hair)

Needles:
4 x 3 mm double-pointed needles or circular needle for magic loop

Other stuff:
Stitch marker
Stuffing
Black embroidery thread and needle (to sew feet and eyes)
Black felt (feet)
2 x seed beads (eyes)
Eerie powers of deduction and the ability to wear the same jumper for days on end
Cardboard
Glue

Skills you'll need:
Knitting in the round. Very basic sewing and embroidery.

Abbreviations:
K = knit
P = purl
Inc1 = increase one (knit into the front and back of a stitch

to make an extra stitch)

K2tog = knit two stitches together

I-cord = idiot cord. Knit stitches on one needle, push to opposite end of needle, knit next row on with yarn pulled tight, repeat.

Pattern:

Little Knitted Sarah Lund is knitted in the round on either double pointed needles (DPN) or a circular needle and magic loop technique. Her head, body and legs are one piece. You add the arms, hair and feet after.

HEAD, BODY AND LEGS

1. Cast on 3 sts in light pink yarn
2. Row 1.inc1 three times (6 sts)
3. Divide sts between three needles, place marker at start of round and join to knit in the round (or divide stitches in half for magic loop)
4. Row 2 and all even rows to Row 10. Knit around
5. Row 3. Inc1 around (12 sts)
6. Row 5. (K, inc1) around (18 sts)
7. Row 7. (K2, inc1) around (24 sts)
8. Row 9. (K3, inc1) around (30 sts)
9. Row 11. (K4, inc1) around (36 sts)
10. Row 12. K around
11. Row 13. K around
12. Row 14. K around
13. Row 15. (K, k2tog) around (24 sts)
14. Row 16. K around
15. Row 17. K around
16. Row 18. (K2, k2tog) around (18 sts)

17. Row 19. K around
18. Row 20. (K, k2tog) around (12 sts)
19. Row 21. K around
20. Row 22. K around
21. Stuff head
22. Row 21. K around
23. Change to cream yarn
24. Row 22. K around
25. Row 23. (K2, p2) around
26. Row 24. Repeat Row 23
27. Row 25. (K, inc1) around (18 sts)
28. Row 26. K around
29. Row 27. (K2, inc1) around (24 sts)
30. Row 28. K around
31. Row 29 to 32. Knit as chart changing between cream and black yarn
32. Row 33 to 36. K around
33. Row 37 to 40. Knit as chart changing between cream and black yarn
34. Row 41 to 44. Change to cream yarn. K around
35. Row 45 and 46. (K2, p2) around
36. Change to blue yarn
37. Row 47 to 56. K around
38. Bind off

ARMS (MAKE TWO)

1. Cast on 4 sts in pink yarn on one DPN or circular needle
2. Push 2 sts to other end of needle
3. Knit 3 rows as i-cord
4. Change to cream yarn
5. Knit 4 rows as i-cord

6. Change to black yarn
7. Knit 1 row as i-cord
8. Change to cream yarn
9. Knit 4 rows as i-cord
10. Change to black yarn
11. Knit 1 row as i-cord
12. Change to cream yarn
13. Knit 4 rows as i-cord
14. Cut yarn leaving a long tail, thread through sts and pull tight
15. Darn in all yarn ends except cast-off tail (which you will use to sew arm to body).

HAIR

1. Cut a 10 cm square of cardboard. Wrap brown yarn around it 30 times.
2. Cut bottom of each loop to make 30 x 10 cm strands keeping them together in one bunch with all the ends even.
3. Cover top of head where hair will be with fabric glue.
4. Place middle of strands on the centre of the head and arrange down the sides and back of the head to form the hair.
5. When glue is dry use black yarn to tie hair into low ponytail. Tie around a few times and tuck in.
6. Use brown yarn to sew a parting slightly to the left side of her head.
7. Sew in a few more strands approx. 12 cm long and knotted at front of parting to make fly-away fringe.

FINISHING

1. Stuff the body but not legs.
2. Using cast-off end from legs sew up middle of legs to make two tubes stopped about 1 cm from the top.
3. Stuff both legs.
4. Use tail from arms to sew arms to body at shoulder height.
5. Cut small felt ovals for feet.
6. Sew circles onto legs using black thread.
7. Embroider ears by using light pink yarn to sew into one stitch on each side of head 8 times.
8. Embroider nose by using light pink yarn to sew into one stitch in the middle of the face 6 times.
9. Sew on seed beads for eyes.
10. Get her a cup of tea. She's going to need it.
11. Optional for folks who want the perfect jumper: embroider dot in middle of square on jumper with black yarn to make a circle.
12. Embroider down arrow above circle and up arrow below with black yarn.
13. Your Little Knitted Sarah Lund lives!

Tips

Add authenticity to Little Knitted Sarah Lund by putting her on a plane to Sweden and removing her just before take-off several times. Watch out for sneaky knife-wielders, Sarah's little jumper isn't armour, you know. Tie Sarah's arms into a stubborn folded position for extra tenaciousness.

Little Knitted Killer (Season 2)
by Lauren O'Farrelll otherwise know as @deadlyknitshade

Just who is our Little Knitted Killer from Season 2? Start stitching to find out, but be careful. Killers are very dangerous when there are pointy sticks around. You'll have to keep an eye on them.

Materials:

8g Light pink DK yarn (skin)
8g Black DK yarn (top and hair)
5g Blue DK yarn (jeans)
Small amount Grey DK yarn (hair)

Needles:

4 x 3 mm double-pointed knitting needles (DPN) or 1 x circular needle for magic loop

Other stuff:

Stitch marker
Stuffing
Black embroidery thread and needle (to sew feet and eyes)
Black felt (feet)
2 x seed beads (eyes)
Murderous intent and sneakiness
Fabric glue

Gauge/Size:

Mot important. Size: approximately 18 cm

Skills you'll need:

Knitting in the round. Very basic sewing and embroidery.

Pattern:

Little Knitted Killer is knitted in the round on double pointed needles (DPN) or using a circular needle and magic loop technique. Her head, body and legs are one piece. You add the arms, hair and feet after.

HEAD, BODY AND LEGS

1. Cast on 3 sts in light pink yarn
2. Row 1.Inc1 three times (6 sts)
3. Divide sts between three needles, place marker at start of round and join to knit in the round (or divide stitches in half for magic loop).
4. Row 2 and all even rows to Row 10. K around
5. Row 3. Inc1 around (12 sts)
6. Row 5. (K, inc1) around (18 sts)
7. Row 7. (K2, inc1) around (24 sts)
8. Row 9. (K3, inc1) around (30 sts)
9. Row 11. (K4, inc1) around (36 sts)
10. Row 12 to 14. K around
11. Row 15. (K, k2tog) around (24 sts)
12. Row 16 and 17. K around
13. Row 18.(K2, k2tog) around (18 sts)
14. Row 19. K around
15. Row 20. (K, k2tog) around (12 sts)
16. Row 21 and 22. K around
17. Stuff head
18. Row 23 and 24. K around
19. Change to black yarn
20. Row 25 and 26. K around
21. Row 27. (K, inc1) around (18 sts)
22. Row 28. K around

23. Row 29. (K2, inc1) around (24 sts)
24. Row 30 to 48. K around
25. Change to blue yarn
26. Row 49 to 60. K around
27. Bind off

ARMS (MAKE TWO)

1. Cast on 4 sts in pink yarn on one dpn or circular needle.
2. Push 2 sts to other end of needle
3. Knit 3 rows as i-cord
4. Change to black yarn
5. Knit 14 rows as i-cord
6. Cut yarn with long tail, thread through sts and pull tight
7. Darn in all yarn ends except cast-off tail (which you will use to sew arm to body)

HAIR

1. Take a small amount of grey yarn and cut into tiny 1 mm pieces till you have a small pile of fluff.
2. Cover top of head where hair will be with fabric glue. You should cover the back and sides of the head with a V shape on top with the point in the middle.
3. Carefully place fluff for hair onto glue and pat and smooth it down to fill all the gaps and make a close-shave haircut.

FINISHING

1. Stuff body but not legs.
2. Using cast-off end from legs sew up middle of legs to make two tubes stopped about 1cm from the top.
3. Stuff both legs.
4. Use tail from arms to sew arms to body at shoulder height.
5. Cut small felt ovals for feet.
6. Sew circles onto legs using black thread.
7. Embroider ears by using light pink yarn to sew into one stitch on each side of head 8 times.
8. Embroider nose by using light pink yarn to sew into one stitch in the middle of the face 6 times.
9. Sew on seed beads for eyes.
10. Back slowwwwly away. He might have it in for you.
11. Your Little Knitted Killer lives! Run away!

Tips:

Feel free to ask your Little Knitted Killer where he was on the night of the murder while shining a spotlight in his face. Don't let your Little Knitted Killer go unwatched. He's a tricky one.

The Sarah Lund Cross Stitch

Perhaps knitting isn't your thing? Perhaps you prefer embroidery? Well lock and load your needles because Louisa Cudahy has come up with this brilliant Sarah Lund cross stitch.

Number	Description	Strands:	Knots	Beads	No.	
DMC 3371	Black Brown	2	0	0		5335
DMC 801	Coffee Brown dark	2	0	0		374
DMC 613	Drab Brown very ligh	2	0	0		46
DMC 920	Copper medium	2	0	0		617
DMC 3854	Autumn Gold medium	2	0	0		1080

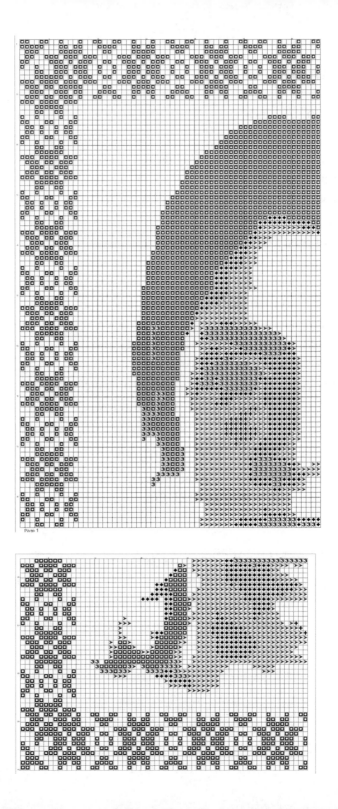

Рисунок 1

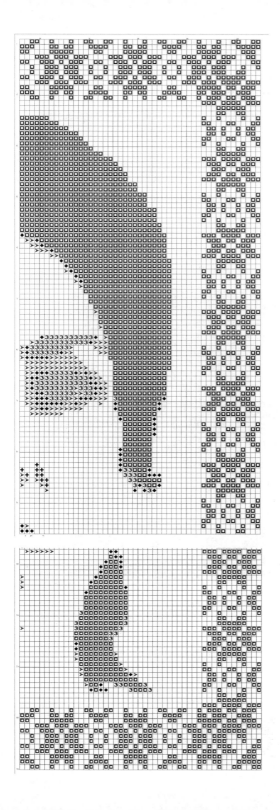

A Jumper For Sofie

Imagine the glorious honour of knitting Sofie Gråbøl a jumper. Well that's a giddy glory I gave one knitter on Twitter. I ran a competition and asked people to send in their best *Killing*-based craft. The winner would get the chance to knit Sofie a jumper. So here are the results:

In third place, it was Jenny Howard and her Red Herring Jumper.

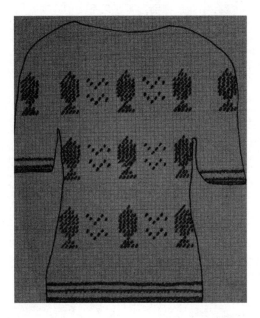

In second it was Lucy Squirrel and her amazing Murder on the Dance Floor rug.

But in first, it was Kathy Calmejane and her extraordinary Gun Cosy.

And if you'd like to recreate Kathy's jumper and have the same jumper as Sofie, then here's the pattern.

Strawberries and Crime

by Kathy Calmejane

Sizes:

S (M, L, XL, XXL)

Recommended yarn:

Norvège (Bergère de France)

Colours:

Viking (red) (base colour) –
7 (8, 8, 9, 9) x 50g skeins –
980 m / 1071 yrds (1120 /
1224 – 1120 / 1224 – 1260 /
1377 – 1260 / 1377)
Glaçon (white) (accent
colour) – 1 (2, 2, 2, 3) x 50g
skeins – 140 m / 153 yrds (280 / 306 – 280 / 306 – 280 / 306
– 420 / 459)

Gauge/swatch:

10 cm of stockinette = 20 sts x 26 rows

Needles:

4 mm knitting needles[1] + 4 mm circular needles (40 – 60
cm length)

Note:

In this pattern, red is used as the base colour and white as
the accent colour. You can of course use whatever colours
you like so, in the instructions, the colours will be called base
and accent rather than red and white.

STRAWBERRIES AND CRIME
by Kathy Calmejane
Finished sizes (after blocking) – all measurements in cm

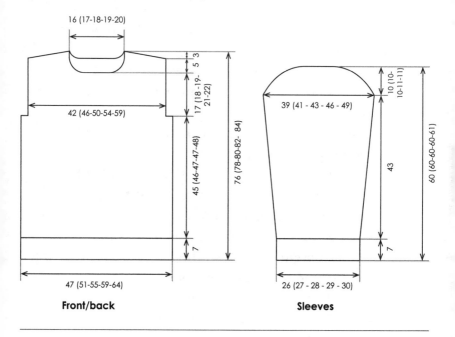

Front/back

Sleeves

Fair-isle pattern charts

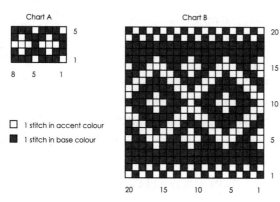

Chart A

Chart B

☐ 1 stitch in accent colour

■ 1 stitch in base colour

BACK

....

1. Cast on 96 (104-112-120-130) sts in base colour and knit in 2-2 rib (k2, p2) for 18 rows (7 cm).
2. Next row: k1, inc. 1, then knit to end of row.
3. Purl all next row.
4. Begin fair-isle pattern chart A[2], starting at st 1 and repeat until end of row. Continue until you reach the top of chart A (5 rows).
5. Work straight in stockinette in base colour until back is 30 cm (78 rows) total length.
6. k1[3], then begin chart A, starting on RS at stitch 1 and repeat until end of row, working last stitch in base colour. Continue until you reach the top of chart A (5 rows)
7. Work 2 rows plain stockinette in base colour.
8. p1, then begin chart B, starting on WS at stitch 10 (6-6-9-10) and repeat until end of row. Continue until you reach the top of chart B (20 rows.
9. Work 2 rows plain stockinette in base colour.
10. k1, then begin chart A, starting on RS at stitch 1 and repeat until end of row. Continue until you reach the top of chart A (5 rows)
11. Continue knitting straight in stockinette in the base colour until total length is 52 (53-54-54-55) cm.
12. At the beginning of the next 2 rows, bind off 6 sts to form the armholes. Continue in stockinette on 85 (93-101-109-119) remaining stitches.
13. k1, then begin chart A, starting at stitch 2 (2-2-2-2) and repeat until end of row. Continue until you reach the top of chart A (5 rows).
14. At 22 (23-24-26-27) cm armhole height, with RS facing,

begin shoulders & neck shaping as follows:

a. Bind off 5 (6-6-7-8) sts, then k 28 (30-33-35-38) sts and place on a stitch holder. The 2 sides will be continued separately.

b. Bind off the next 19 (21-23-25-27) sts to form the neck. Work to end.

c. Armhole side: bind off 5 (6-6-7-8) sts, work to end

d. Neck side: bind off 3 st, work to end.

e. Armhole side: bind off 5 (6-6-7-8) sts, work to end

f. Neck side: bind off 2 sts, work to end.

g. Armhole side: bind off 5 (6-6-7-8) sts, work to end

h. Neck side: bind off 1 st, work to end.

i. Armhole side: bind off 6 (6-7-7-8) sts, work to end

j. Work 1 row straight.

k. Bind off remaining stitches.

l. With WS facing, pick up stitches from holder and repeat steps d to k to form other side of neck and shoulders.

FRONT

1. Repeat steps 1 – 13 for back.

2. In step 8 of Back instructions begin chart B at stitch 6 (6-6-9-10) on WS.

3. At 17 (18-19-21-22) cm armhole height, with RS facing, begin shoulders and neck shaping as follows:

   a. When raglan is 15 (16-18-19-20) cm high, k14 and place those stitches on stitch holder.

   a. Knit 35 (38-41-44-48) sts and place on a stitch holder. The 2 sides will be continued separately.

   b. Bind off the next 15 (17-19-21-23) sts to form the neck. Work to end.

c. Work 1 row straight

d. Neck side: bind off 3 sts, work to end.

e. Work 1 row straight

f. Neck side: bind off 2 sts, work to end.

g. Work 1 row straight.

h. Neck side: bind off 1 st, work to end.

i. Work 1 row straight

j. Repeat steps h. and i. once.

k. Neck side: bind off 1 st, work to end.

l. Armhole side: bind off 5 (6-6-7-8) sts, work to end

m. Work 1 row straight.

n. Repeat steps l. and m. once

o. Armhole side: bind off 5 (6-7-7-8) sts, work to end

p. Work 1 row straight.

q. Armhole side: bind off 6 (6-7-7-8) sts, work to end

r. Work 1 row straight.

s. Bind off remaining stitches.

4. With WS facing, pick up stitches from holder and repeat steps b. to s. to form other side of neck and shoulders.

SLEEVES (MAKE TWO)

1. Cast on 54 (56-58-60-62) sts and work in double rib (k2, p2, repeat until end of row. In following rows, work stitches as they come) until cuff is 7 cm (18 rows) long.

2. Knit all the next row, purl the following row, then begin chart A, starting at stitch 1.

3. After the 5th row of chart A is completed, purl the next row.

4. Next row (increase row): k2, inc.1, knit until 2 sts remain, inc.1, k2.

5. Continue working in stockinette stitch, repeating step

4 every 8 (6-6-6-4) rows until you have increased 13 (14-15-17-19) times in total (including row in step 4)[4]. After all increase rows are done, you should have a total of 78 (82-86-92-98) sts.

6. At The Same Time: While repeating increase rows as above, when sleeve is 35 cm long:

   a. Begin chart A (starting on RS at st 1), continue until you reach the top of chart A (5 rows).

   b. Work 2 rows in stockinette in base colour.

   c. Begin chart B, starting on WS at stitch 9 (11-12-9-11),continue until you reach the top of chart B (20 rows).

   d. Work 2 rows in stockinette in base colour.

   e. Begin chart A (starting on RS at st 1), continue until you reach the top of chart A (5 rows).

7. After last increase row, continue in stockinette in base colour until sleeve is 50 cm long from cast-on edge.

8. Bind off 3 sts at the beginning of the next 6 rows. Bind off 2 sts at the beginning of the next 14 (14-14-16-16) rows, then bind off 3 sts at beginning of next 4 rows.

9. Bind off remaining 20 (24-28-30-36) sts.

COLLAR

1. Cast on 124 (128-132-136-140) sts on circular needles and work in the round: *k2, p2* repeat * to * until collar is 5 cm high.

2. Change to a contrasting colour yarn and bind off. This cast off will be unravelled when assembling so use a yarn that will be easy to pull out. Leave a long tail of base colour yarn when changing, so that it can be used to assemble collar.

Alternative for straight needles: Cast on 2 more sts. than indicated above and knit as above ending with an extra k2 at the end of first line. Knit double ribbing until piece is 7 cm long, then cast off with contrasting yarn as above. When assembling, sew the 2 short ends together first then assemble as directed.

Alternative for turtleneck collar: Continue the collar until it is 18 cm long to allow for fold over.

FINISHING

1. Block to measurements on chart. This step is important as it will relax the yarn, especially in the fair-isle pattern sections, and allow you to check that your jumper will fit correctly. Allow all sections to cool and dry completely before assembling.
2. Sew side seams, using either a backstitch or invisible/ mattress stitch. Graft shoulder seams together.
3. Sew sleeve seams, using either a backstitch or invisible/ mattress stitch.
4. Fit a shoulder cap into each armhole and sew on.
5. To assemble collar, thread your needle with the tail of base colour yarn from the collar and begin undoing contrasting cast-off one stitch at a time. Alternately slip your sewing needle into the neckline of the main body and through the stitches of the collar as they become free from the cast-off yarn.
6. Secure and weave in all ends.

Tips

1. Knitting fair-isle is very much a question of tension. The large fair-isle section in the middle of this jumper

is designed to be slightly tighter than the main body to create a more feminine shape. For a looser fit, or if you tend to knit quite tight, switch to 4.5 mm needles when doing the pattern sections.

2. The pattern strip at the bottom of the jumper needs to be quite elastic to ensure a good fit. If you tend to knit tightly, you can knit this part in the base colour in stockinette and embroider the pattern on after finishing. Alternatively, you can switch to size 4.5 mm needles for this section.

3. For all pattern rows, the stitch indicated to start with will always be worked on the 2nd stitch of your row. For a nice, regular edge, always leave the first and last stitch of every row "plain", in the base colour. This will make assembling easier. When starting or ending a colour pattern section, knit the first stitch with both yarns together to secure the end.

4. If you don't have any row markers or counters to keep track of how many increases you have made, hook a short strand of contrasting yarn through the first stitch of each increase row to make them easier to spot. Tie the strand in a loose knot, and don't forget to remove before assembling!

Glossary

Stockinette: alternating rows of knit and purl.

RS: Right Side, the 'flat' side, when knitting in stockinette. When knitting fair-isle, this is the side the pattern will show on.

WS: Wrong Side, the 'lumpy' side of stockinette. When knitting the fair-isle pattern, the trailing yarns should all be on this side.

kX: knit X stitches

pX: purl X stitches

inc: increase (make an extra stitch) - one simple method is to insert the needle into the top loop of the stitch below the next one on your needle and knit this as a regular stitch, then knit the next stitch normally.

sts: stitches

Work to end: continue knitting or purling stitches as they appear until the end of the row.

Ribbing or 2-2 rib: when you alternate an amount of knit and purl stitches (for example 2-2 rib means k2, p2) and continue working these stitches as they come forming vertical 'stripes' that cause the fabric to bunch up, this is called ribbing. It is mainly used to gather fabric around the cuffs, neckline and the bottom of a sweater.

Raglan: a raglan is the sloping shape given to the front, back and sleeves from under the arms to the neckline.

11

WONDERFUL, WONDERFUL COPENHAGEN

So now you're in command of everything you need to know to take yourself to Copenhagen and begin your *Forbrydelsen* pilgrimage. But just where are all those iconic places you have grown to love?

1 CITY HALL

Location: *City Hall Square, off Vester Voldgade*
Construction on City Hall began in 1892 and it was opened in 1905. Its iconic clock tower stands 105.6 metres tall and is one of the highest points in Copenhagen. It's also the home of Jens Olsen's World Clock, an astronomical clock with a perpetual calendar which can also show solar and lunar eclipses.

2 CHRISTIANSBORG PALACE

Location: *Prins Jørgens Gård, Slotsholmen*
Home of the Folketing, the Danish Parliament, this is where the political shenanigans in Series 2 and 3 take place. It's also the home of Borgen but wevvers to that. The first castle was

built on this site in 1157. It's been burnt down twice, in 1794 and 1884; and the most recent additions to the architecture were completed in 1928.

3 KANALCAFEEN

Location: *Fredericksholms Kanal 18*

This is where Lund goes for a quick supper with Troels. It's also where Bengt, her boyfriend, sits and gets wasted waiting in vain for her to join him for supper before driving off in a huff and breaking his arm and banging his head. The Swedish idiot.

4 POLICE HQ

Location: *Polititorvet 1*

Where it's ALL happening. You need a special pass to enter, but sometimes kind guards do let you have a quick peek inside.

5 RYVANGEN MEMORIAL PARK

Location: *5 km from central Copenhagen, Mindelunden I Ryvangen, Hellerup*

Scene of the first murder in Series 2. The place where Anne Dragsholm is discovered and where the series finale plays out. Stand on the very mound where Lund is shot.

The park was established in 1945 after the Nazis retreated from Denmark. The site is significant because it was the place the Nazis used to murder members of the Danish Resistance. After the Nazis left, the bodies of hundreds of Danish Resistance fighters were found and reburied with full honours.

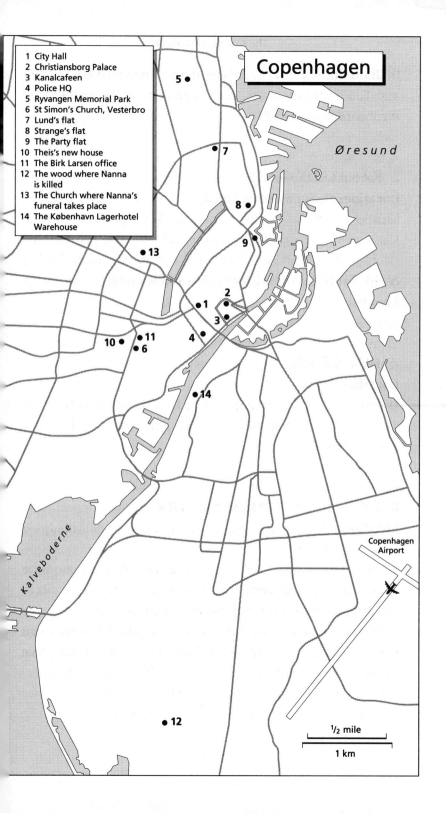

1 City Hall
2 Christiansborg Palace
3 Kanalcafeen
4 Police HQ
5 Ryvangen Memorial Park
6 St Simon's Church, Vesterbro
7 Lund's flat
8 Strange's flat
9 The Party flat
10 Theis's new house
11 The Birk Larsen office
12 The wood where Nanna
   is killed
13 The Church where Nanna's
   funeral takes place
14 The København Lagerhotel
   Warehouse

Copenhagen

Øresund

5 •

7 •

8 •

9 •

13 •

1 •

2 •

3 •

10 • 11 •
    • 6

4 •

14 •

Kalveboderne

Copenhagen
Airport

12 •

¹/₂ mile

1 km

The execution pole that Anne Dragsholm is tied to is also significant, in that the Nazis used three execution poles during 1943 – 5 to kill Resistance fighters. The original posts have been preserved in bronze and it's to one of these that Anne Drasholm is tied.

Because of the sensitive nature of the site, they recreated the execution poles and filmed those scenes at another location.

6 ST SIMON'S CHURCH, VESTERBRO

Location: *KRISTKIRKEN, Enghave Plads 18, 1670 København V.*

Home of Priest and the 3-2-Alpha survivors who hop tentatively in like rabbits negotiating their way around a foxhole.

7 LUND'S FLAT

Location: *Østerbrogade 95*

Everyone has stood outside Lund's flat waiting in the shadows for her – Troels, Strange, they've all done it. Now so can you.

8 STRANGE'S FLAT

Location: *Kristianiagade*

And here it is, the home of a ruthless killer. Let the chills run down your spine as you recall that moment he almost got a snog in. Brrrrrrrrr.

9 THE PARTY FLAT
Location: *130 Store Kongengsgade*
Where the whole mess started. Stand in the same spot Nanna Birk Larsen asked Jens Holck for the keys and despair. Actually – the courtyard scenes are filmed a bit further up the street, so why not wander in and see if you can find it . . .

10 THEIS'S NEW HOUSE
Location: *Küchlersgade, Vesterbro*
Grisly scenes took place here. Not only is it where Nanna Birk Larsen is held and raped over 24 hours, but it's the scene of the greatest clue reveal in history – 'SARAJEVO 84'. Look but don't touch, though – don't get any funny ideas about busting in a door window using a brick and then tearing up the floorboards in the basement. They won't like that.

11 THE BIRK LARSEN OFFICE
Location: *Frederikstade, Vesterbro*
This was actually a set in studio but they intended the location to be just round the corner from the new house, so if you walk nearby Frederikstade, that's where it would have been.

12 THE WOOD WHERE NANNA IS KILLED
Location: *Whitsun Forest, Pinseskoven*
Brrrrr, Brrrrr a thousand times Brrrrrrr

13 THE CHURCH WHERE NANNA'S FUNERAL TAKES PLACE

Location: *on the corner of Rantzausgade and J. Brochmands Gade*

Sit in the very pews where Pernille, Theis and the boys said their final farewell. Boo very hoo.

14 THE KØBENHAVN LAGERHOTEL WAREHOUSE

Location: *Islands Brygge, just after Dreschelsgade.*

The warehouse where Mette Hauge's stuff is stored and Meyer is shot.

12

SERIES THREE

Here's my advice. If you don't want to read one single thing about what to expect in Series 3 then put this book down now. Leave it where it lies. Walk away, open a door, feel the sun on your face. It's going to be all right.

Don't worry, there are no spoilers here; but I am going to give you a run-down on what to expect. Ten one-hour episodes are now all that's left to you. *Forbrydelsen III* is the very last series. There shall be no more.

The Plot

It's three years later. Europe is in economic crisis, and so is Denmark.

Sarah Lund, now 46, has been promoted to Detective Chief Inspector, but 25 years with the force have taken their toll and she wants to leave Homicide and move to another department with more regular hours and desk work.

She's moved to a new house and is looking to find some happiness before life passes her by.

She's also got a newJumper.

She's teamed up with a new, idealistic Detective Constable

called Juncker (Sigurd Holmen le Dous). The body of what appears to be a homeless man has been found in a rubbish dump and Lund gives the case a low priority before realizing that it's the prelude to a much larger, important case that is going to have far-reaching ramifications for all of Denmark. A child has been kidnapped. And it's Lund's job to find her.

As for the politics, we're back at parliament where the Prime Minister, Kristian Kamper, is preparing the final days of his campaign for re-election. Denmark's economy, the Prime Minister's political future and the case become intertwined and Lund comes under increased pressure to solve it as quickly as possible.

That's it. I'm not telling you another single thing. What I can tell you, however, is who the main characters are going to be. So, apart from Lund and Brix and Ruth Hedeby, it's all new faces. And here they are.

✲ Kristian Kamper (Olaf Johannessen)

The incumbent Prime Minister. The election is in ten days' time. At the beginning of the series, Kamper's chances of being re-elected are good, but a series of smears turn the tide against him.

✲ Robert Zeuthen (Anders W. Berthelsen)

The business magnate whose daughter has been kidnapped. Is he going to keep his billions in Denmark? Or leave for ever?

✲ *Fun Fact:* Anders broke his leg between filming Episodes 1 and 2. During Episodes 2, 3 and 4 keep your eye out for Anders walking into shot and standing very still. He's also replaced by a stuntman for all his walking and running shots.

Anders says: *'I was delighted because I am rubbish at running. I look like a girl running.'*

✳ HC (Nikolaj Kaas)
From PET, the Danish version of Special Branch, HC is teamed up with Lund to crack the case.

✳ Juncker (Sigurd Holmen Le Dous)
The young rookie detective whom Lund is tasked to mentor.

✳ Karen Nebel (Trine Pallesen)
Kamper's spin doctor.

✳ Maja Zeuthen (Helle Fagralid)
Divorced wife of Robert Zeuthen, mother of the kidnapped child.

And that's ALL I'm giving you. Now let's see how much you *really* know about *Forbrydelsen* . . . turn the page *if you dare.*

13

THE HARDEST, MOST IMPOSSIBLE QUIZ EVER

Think you know everything there is to know about *The Killing*? Then why not try out your skills on this Über Difficult Test. It's fiendish. GOOD LUCK!

The Killing Quiz

SERIES 1

1. How old is Anna Hartmann when she dies?

2. How old is Nanna Birk Larsen when she's killed?

3. What percentage is the rise in absenteeism from schools since Bremer has cut funding to maintaining school buildings?

4. What's the name of Mark's hockey team?

5. Who did Nanna go to the Halloween party dressed as?

6. What's the name of Nanna's school?

7. Who is in charge of the Volunteers at City Hall?

8. What's the numberplate of the car Nanna has been found dead in?

9. What is found clenched in Nanna's fist?

10. What's the name of the blind lady's cat?

11. What's Sarah Lund's mother's name?

12. How much does Sarah Lund weigh?

13. What time every day does Morten meditate?

14. What's the name of the news agency that puts out the story of the campaign car being connected to the murder?

15. Who is the President of the Student Council?

16. What's the restaurant owner whom Theis goes to visit called?

17. Name the Birk Larsen 'boys'.

18. What subject does Rahman teach?

19. What's the name of the teacher writing the paper on trends in language?

20. What books did Nanna return to Rahman?

21. Name Sarah Lund's boyfriend.

22. What's his job?

23. Name the man in charge of the Liberal Group who tries to oust Troels.

24. Name Rahman's accomplice.

25. Name the leader of the Moderates.

26. Name Bremer's advisor.

27. What's the address of the Party flat?

28. What's the name Lund uses for her fake profile on the Boils dating website?

29. What's Faust's profile tagline?

30. Name the woman Troels has an affair with (bonus point for her online name).

31. What are the three topics Bremer chooses when he changes the agenda to reveal disharmony amongst those seeking an alliance against him?

32. Name Lund's ex–husband.

33. How much extra money was Olav Christensen getting every month?

34. And what was the money officially for?

35. How many calls were made to Nanna from Latvia?

36. Name the first woman killed by Vagn.

37. And what was the name of the removal firm that Vagn used to work for?

38. Who owns that company?

39. What is the name of the crucial document referred to in the minutes of the meeting between Bremer and Stokke?

40. Name the journalist who is closing in on Toiletgate.

41. What is the name of the storage warehouse where Mette's things are being kept?

42. And what number unit is Mette's?

43. What does Lund arm herself with in the warehouse?

44. Name Meyer's children.

45. What stopped the second bullet that went into Meyer?

46. Name the school Vagn and Mette went to together.

47. What is Pernille's sister called?

48. Where does Vagn tell Theis he's getting a puppy from?

49. Is Vagn left- or right-handed?

50. Where is Sarah Lund supposed to be moving to in Sweden?

SERIES 2

51. Name the Minister for Justice who has to be replaced.

52. What important bill is Buch tasked with seeing through parliament?

53. Where is Sarah Lund now working?

54. Name Thomas Buch's private secretary.

55. Name the leader of the People's Party.

56. Name the lawyer who has been found dead at the beginning of the series.

57. How many times has she been stabbed?

58. Where has her body been found?

59. Name the Deputy Commissioner.

60. What's Sarah Lund's mother's boyfriend called?

61. And what is he allergic to?

62. What does Sarah Lund buy Mark for his birthday?

63. What clue does Sarah Lund spot at the birthday party?

64. What's the name of the organization credited for making the video that's released on the internet?

65. Name the head of Special Branch.

66. Name the Head of Barracks.

67. What's Raben's wife called?

68. What are the two things Strange tells Lund he likes?

69. What is the pen name of the person sending emails to Kodmani?

70. How does Raben escape from jail?

71. Name the task force sent to Afghanistan.

72. Name the squadron headed up by Raben.

73. Name the second victim.

74. Name the political group the People's Party want banned.

75. What's David Gruner's job?

76. How was the fire that killed David Gruner started?

77. What is round Gruner's neck when his body is found?

78. Name the hotel Monberg went to to have his affair.

79. Name the army barracks.

80. Where has Lisbeth Thomsen gone to live?

81. What prevents Lund and Strange taking Lisbeth Thomsen from the island?

82. What has been stolen from the barracks?

83. How does Lisbeth Thomsen die?

84. What is the name of the mysterious officer that Lund is trying to find?

85. Name the Minister for Defence.

86. Whose body does Lund have dug up?

87. What does Lund receive at the wedding?

88. Which church does the Priest work at?

89. What's above the meat-processing unit?

90. What pizza do Lund and Strange order?

91. What is it about the severed hand which means it can't have belonged to a suicide bomber?

92. What piece of fruit does Buch eat because he's eaten 'too many sweets'?

93. Where is Carsten Plough being sent?

94. Name the army surgeon Lund goes to visit.

95. Name Colonel Jarnvig's boss.

96. Where does Lund find the bodies of the family killed in the atrocity?

97. Who kidnaps Louise?

98. Where did Dragsholm see Strange and why did she start asking questions?

99. How many times does Strange shoot Lund?

100. How many times does Lund shoot Strange?

ANSWERS

1. 39
2. 19
3. 20%
4. KSF
5. Madam Mim from *Donald Duck*
6. Frederiksholm
7. Rikke Nielsen
8. XU 24 919
9. A black heart necklace
10. Samson
11. Vibeke
12. 57.2 kg
13. Between 5.30 and 6 p.m.
14. Ritzau
15. Jeppe Hald
16. Karim
17. Anton and Emil
18. Danish
19. Henning Kofoed
20. Two Karen Blixen books
21. Bengt Rosling

22. Criminal Profiler
23. Knud Padde
24. Mustafa Akkad
25. Jens Holck
26. Phillip Dessau
27. 4th floor, 130 Store Kongensgade
28. Janne Meyer
29. Ruling the heart can be the most difficult thing
30. Nethe Stjernfeldt (Fanny Hill)
31. Harbour Tunnel, Congestion Charge, Drug Dens
32. Carsten
33. 500 Kroner
34. Environmental reports
35. 21
36. Mette Hauge
37. Merkur
38. Edel Lonstrup
39. Appendix 13X
40. Erik Salin
41. København Lagerhotel
42. 554
43. A candlestick
44. Ella, Neel, Marie
45. His cigarette lighter
46. Fuglegaards
47. Lotte
48. Poland
49. Both. He shoots the gun with his right hand and writes the birthday card with his left.
50. Sigtuna
51. Frode Monberg
52. The Terrorism Package

53. In Gedser
54. Karina Munk Jørgensen
55. Erling Krabbe
56. Anne Dragsholm
57. 21
58. Memorial Park
59. Ruth Hedeby
60. Bjørn
61. Nuts
62. A hooded top
63. A cellophane wrapper from a film cassette
64. Muslim Leagus
65. Erik Konig
66. Colonel Torsten Jarnvig
67. Louise
68. Football and opera
69. Faith Fellow
70. He uses wire-cuttters to break into a manhole
71. Team Aegir
72. 3-2-Alpha Squad
73. Myg Poulson
74. Ahl Al Kahf
75. He's a security guard
76. The explosive device was activated by a mobile phone
77. A rubber tyre
78. Hotel Hammersloj
79. Ryvangen Army Barracks
80. The Swedish island of Skogo
81. There's a roadblock of logs
82. 5 kilos of plastic explosives
83. Her boat explodes when she turns on the motor
84. Perk

85. Rossing
86. Per K Moller
87. A bunch of flowers
88. St Simon's Church, Vesterbro
89. A nightclub
90. A number 38 (with extra cheese)
91. It is covered in a henna tattoo and is wearing a gold ring. The Taliban don't wear gold and the henna tattoo is from the Hazara tribe, who are the enemies of the Taliban.
92. A small pear
93. To Skopje
94. Frederik Holst
95. General Arild
96. In an old bread oven
97. Bilal
98. At a court hearing. It was hot and Strange was wearing a teeshirt. She saw his tattoo.
99. Four
100. Ten

How did you get on?

If you got **10 – 20** questions right then well done, you were paying attention; but call yourself a fan? Come on!

21 – 30: Your attention to small details is admirable. Pat yourself on the back.

30 – 49: You've probably spent hours on internet chat rooms discussing *The Killing* ad nauseam. I salute you.

50 - 99: Put down this book and go out for a walk. You need to reassess your life and priorities.

100: Congratulations, you win Sofie Gråbøl!

And that's that. If you have any still-unanswered plot questions then why not ask me? You can contact me on Twitter @EmmaK67.

Enjoy Series 3!

Tak!

Thanks

It's been an amazing privilege to write this book and there are a host of people I need to thank for making it possible. Firstly, my editor Jane Sturrock, who asked me to do it in the first place; you have given me the greatest Christmas present imaginable. Secondly, my wonderful agent, Sheila Crowley, whose unflappable calm sees me through every storm. Thirdly, to Drew Meakin and Sarah Delaney who told me everything I needed to know about Danish interior design. And fourthly, to all the magnificent actors who gave their time to me and didn't mind that I was so over-excited. But my greatest and most heartfelt thanks must go to Piv Bernth, the Producer, and Sofie Gråbøl, who have welcomed me with open arms and made me feel part of the *Forbrydelsen* Family. Your friendship has been overwhelming. I bloody love you.

Emma Kennedy is an actress, *Sunday Times* bestselling writer and Celebrity Masterchef Champion 2012 who has appeared in many award-winning comedy shows including Goodness Gracious Me and *The Smoking Room*. She has been writing for Radio 4 and 2 for over a decade and is the author of bestselling books *The Tent, The Bucket and Me* and *I Left My Tent in San Francisco*.